Praise for *Against Erasure*

"At a time of an unfolding Israeli genocide against 2.3 million Palestinians in Gaza, enabled as much by racist, dehumanizing propaganda as by Western arms, funds, and colonial complicity, it is more important than ever to always remember to see the human behind the number, the oppression behind the violence, and the complicity behind the genocide. This precious book shares a glimpse of Palestinian lives prior to the Nakba, the initial destruction of our beautiful homeland to project an image of a 'desert' that needs a white colonial settler to make it bloom. In the face of this excruciatingly painful phase of our ongoing Nakba of ruthless, inherently supremacist, settler-colonial conquest, celebrating our heritage, our cultural roots, our love for life, for freedom, for justice becomes more necessary than ever. This book helps us do so."
—OMAR BARGHOUTI, Palestinian human rights defender and cofounder of the BDS movement for Palestinian rights

"*Against Erasure* is a stunning demonstration of Palestinian resistance and joy, as well as the beautiful persistence of our people. As argument, it documents the thriving existence of families, children, and whole communities before Nakba, illustrating our powerful connection to the homeland, which persists and resists until full liberation. This book is a testament to the schools we once occupied and the orange groves our great-grandfathers planted. Through this book, we look into the past as a means of creating and charging toward a future of return."
—NOOR HINDI, author of *Dear God. Dear Bones. Dear Yellow.*

"We live in a moment when Palestinian life is being ruthlessly dehumanized in the service of a looming genocide. *Against Erasure: A Photographic Memory of Palestine before the Nakba* is not only beautiful and heart-wrenching. It is a political reminder that we are fighting not only for Palestinian life but against an erasure of their entire history."
—Dave Zirin, sports editor of *The Nation*

Against Erasure

A Photographic Memory of Palestine before the Nakba

Teresa Aranguren and Sandra Barrilaro

Translated from the Spanish edition by Róisín Davis with Hugo Rayón Aranguren

Foreword by Mohammed El-Kurd

Haymarket Books
Chicago, Illinois

This edition published in 2024 by Haymarket Books, P.O. Box 180165, Chicago, IL 60618
www.haymarketbooks.org, info@haymarketbooks.org

ISBN: 978-1-64259-980-0

Front cover photograph © UNRWA. Back cover photograph © Olga Kattan—Cantarabia Archive. Cover design by Rachel Cohen.
Interior design by Sandra Barrilaro.

Distributed to the trade in the US through Consortium Book Sales and Distribution (www.cbsd.com) and internationally through Ingram Publisher Services International (www.ingramcontent.com).

This book was published with the generous support of Lannan Foundation, Wallace Action Fund, and Marguerite Casey Foundation.

Special discounts are available for bulk purchases by organizations and institutions. Please email info@haymarketbooks.org for more information.

Printed in Canada by union labor.

Library of Congress Cataloging-in-Publication data is available.

10 9 8 7 6 5 4 3 2

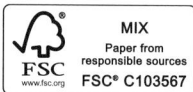

Contents

In these dark days of November 2023, while the final touches are being made to this edition, we're witnessing with horror, powerlessness, and anguish, a new Palestinian Nakba. Israel is mercilessly bombing the population of Gaza and forcing the eviction of more than a million Gazans in a new ethnic cleansing operation similar to that of 1948. As we write these lines, the number of civilians and children killed has entered the tens of thousands. All of this, before the eyes of the world and the shameful passivity of the international community. Meanwhile, the assault on the population of the West Bank, at the hands of settlers and the occupation army is intensifying. In these dark days, more than ever, Palestine is in our hearts and minds. In these dark days we dedicate this book to the people of Palestine: friends and strangers, always human.

Acknowledgments

This book is the result of the generous help of many people. The initial inspiration for the project came from our friend Soheila Atwan, a Palestinian who lives in Madrid, who put us in contact with Professor Mansour and his family in Haifa. During our time in that beautiful Mediterranean city, we enjoyed the friendly, fun, always stimulating company of Jafar Farah, Asmahan Atwan, and filmmaker Ula Tabari; the hospitality of the Mossawa Center directed by Jafar; and the generosity of Professor Mansour, who donated not only his time but many of the photographs that appear in this book. We were fortunate to spend time with Nimer Yazbek from Nazareth, to whom we owe thanks for the use of various photographs from his collection.

For that first trip, we are grateful for the help and warm welcome extended to us by Fayez Saqqa, Aida Slebi, Khaled Al Sa'adi, and Nawaf Hamed, who were our guides in Bethlehem, Ramallah, and Jerusalem against the turbulent backdrop of June 2014 in the West Bank.

We owe a very special thanks to our translators: Jalil Sadaka, Rifaat Atfé, and Adnan Al Ayoubi, who translated the texts from Spanish to Arabic, and to Professor Carmen Ruiz Bravo, who was in charge of the translations from Arabic to Spanish and who also contributed some excellent photographs from the archive of her publishing house, Cantarabia. We also thank Mary C. González Vallejo for her help with translation.

We thank Professor Isaías Barrañeda; Marwan El Burini, president of the Hispano-Palestine Association of Madrid; and the ambassador of Palestine in Spain, Musa Odeh, who from the beginning encouraged us to undertake this project and offered us their contacts and support.

Our thanks to Raquel Martí and the United Nations Relief and Works Agency for Palestine Refugees in the Near East (UNRWA) for their collaboration and for providing the photographs belonging to the archive of UNRWA the that appear in this book.

The confidence that our Spanish publisher, Ediciones del Oriente y del Mediterráneo, demonstrated toward us from the start of the project as well as the solidarity shown to us by the Biladi Association of Euskadi, the Araguaney Foundation of Santiago de Compostela, and the Committee for Solidarity with the Arab Cause, of Asturias, have all made this book possible.

Above all, we owe our gratitude to the people of Palestine, past and present, to those who appear in these photographs and those who do not.

Sandra Barrilaro and Teresa Aranguren

Enough for Me

Enough for me to die on her earth
be buried in her
to melt and vanish into her soil
then sprout forth as a flower
played with by a child from my country.
Enough for me to remain
in my country's embrace
to be in her close as a handful of dust
a sprig of grass
a flower.

*Fadwa Tuqan**

---

* Palestinian poet, born in 1914 in Nablus, where she lived until her death in 2003.

Foreword to the 2024 Edition

I am writing this foreword in English and Arabic, and it is in these moments that the profound chasm between these two languages reveals itself. In English, there is a need to riddle the page with facts and figures detailing the essential cruelties of an atrocity that should be—and should have long been—internationally recognized. I'm tempted to squeeze into these lines a history lesson, to list the names of the various terrorist paramilitaries that formed the Israeli military terrorizing us today; the number of massacres, exiles, refugees; the endless hectares of stolen land; the pregnant bellies split open in Deir Yassin.

There is no need for such contextualization in Arabic: the Nakba breathes down our necks, invading our national identity and contorting our earliest encounters with our sense of self. It is relentless. It happens in the present tense, everywhere on the map. For some households, it began when a grandfather was dispossessed in Jaffa and sought refuge in Gaza, where it continues in the rumble of the warplanes and bombs on the blockaded enclave, introducing his grandchildren to their first—or perhaps third, or sixth—war. Not a corner of our geography is spared, not a generation.[*]

And it is seemingly ubiquitous—following us even in exile. A Palestinian born in Lebanon's Ein El-Hilweh refugee camp, and not in their grandparents' Akka, that is both far and near, less than 100 kilometers away, will live tortured by

---

* When I started writing this in July 2023, hundreds of Palestinians were forced to leave their houses in the Jenin Refugee Camp as an Israeli battalion targeted families, medics, journalists, infrastructure, and guerillas, killing eleven people. The scene bore a harrowing resemblance to an April afternoon in 1948 when thousands—some of whom are now marching alongside those chased out of the camp—were expelled from their original homes in Haifa and dragged by the Haganah into cars that drove them to what would forcibly become their new home: Jenin.

their aborted potentials, deprived of citizenship and right to movement. And it is absurd: settlers with New York accents, armed with rifles and can escape criminal charges in the United States to squat a Jerusalemite's home, backed by their army, judiciary, and God (their favorite real estate agent).*

Still, most, if not all, of this well-documented theft and bloodshed is denied and obfuscated by prominent political, media, and academic institutions in the Anglophone world.

The pioneers of Zionism have invisibilized us since first embarking on their search for a great imperial power to adopt their movement. Before denying the massacres they inflicted on us, they were denying our very existence. The colonial narrative was that our blossoming, biodiverse Palestine was conveniently barren and "without a people,"† and if there were indeed a people, amid the arid plains and the passing tumbleweeds, we were rootless, nomadic‡ and, according to Jabotinsky, "uncivilized."§ We were "the remnants of a nation / scattered across caves."¶ And so the Nakba—the largest armed robbery in modern history—was a gift the Zionists bestowed upon us. The thieves have generously lingered in our living rooms with their feet kicked up. They milk our goats and plant our gardens with cherry tomatoes. They had apparently made the desert bloom and "liberated even the grazing cattle when [they] gave Mohammed's field to Abraham."**

Such colonial mythology has been necessary to orchestrate this extreme case of social engineering. And such mythology is needed for it to continue. While it can be argued that all Palestinians know that the Nakba wasn't a sudden disaster and isn't a tragic relic from the past, I worry that sometimes the Nakba is treated as a one-dimensional event, marked by loss and only loss. The myth that we escaped or surrendered advances the idea that the Zionist settler enterprise in Palestine

---

* As I write this, Rafat Sublaban, whose Old City home was taken over by government-backed settler organizations on July 10, 2023, screams, "We want our furniture," at the settlers taunting him from his very windows, living shamelessly among his hijacked memories and personal belongings.

† Israel Zangwill, *The Return To Palestine* (1901)

‡ Though it must be said that even if Palestine were not "civilized" according to the ethnocentric standards of the Western powers that targeted it, and even if Palestinians were "nomads," Zionist colonization in Palestine would still be indefensible.

§ Ze'ev Jabotinsky, *The Iron Wall: Colonization of Palestine Agreement with Arabs Impossible Zionism Must Go Forward* (1923)

¶ Rashid Hussien, *God Is A Refugee* (1960)

** Hussien first read this poem at the Organization of Arab Farmers' conference in Akka, in protest of the 1960 Israeli "Land Law," which classified 93% of the lands in historic Palestine as "state-owned." The poem also references the 1950 "Absentee Property Law" which allowed the Israeli government to arrogate the properties of Palestinian refugees displaced during the Nakba.

is impenetrable, that resistance is futile and always has been. But Palestinian freedom fighters have long been a thorn in the colonizers' throats, fighting until the very last bullet—much like in recent years, be it in Nablus, Jenin, or Gaza. And much like we have not yet been defeated, Zionism is yet to complete its mission in our homeland.

Before conjuring the ability to write a few coherent paragraphs prefacing this book, all I could think while flipping through these photographs was *What have they done to you? What have they done to Palestine?* I was struck by images of Palestine before the walls and the colonies, and checkpoints clogged its arteries; photos captured between towns and villages, now separated by concrete barriers and pulled worlds apart, that before were intertwined socially and economically. Our eyes seldom encounter Palestine before the Israeli regime; a Palestine not defined by its ailments but defined by its industries and cultures. Yet, it is important to resist the urge to romanticize that era. One must situate these photographs within the proper socio-economic context and ask about what is *not* represented in these images—who had access to cameras? Who was behind those cameras? What can be said of those who lived far from the flashing lights and tape recorders? Where do we look for their fossilized legacies? The tessellate of beautiful, unseen photographs this volume produces is as illuminating as it is incomplete. This book is one of many efforts to archive and document our stories and our grandparents' stories. There are many conversations we should be having with our grandparents, on their dinner tables before their deathbeds, and even more work to do if we are to ensure that the victims and resistors of the present-day Nakba aren't merely acknowledged in fleeting headlines.

Against Erasure reaffirms that Palestine's history does not begin in fleeing. Not only does this book defy the brutal revisionism on the part of the empires and mercenaries seeking to vanquish us, it also disrupts the engineered cultural and political mystification of the Nakba that has, for generations, made its undoing seem impossibly remote.

Mohammed El-Kurd

Foreword to the 2016 Edition

The history of the so-called "Palestinian question" is plagued with forgetting, with falsehoods, contradictions, and misrepresentations, which in the long term contribute to a sort of "anti-history," a pseudohistory with little bearing on the realities of what has come to pass. I use "plagued" here deliberately for its etymological meaning, because in historicizing the Palestinian question, we encounter just that: a veritable plague, a disgrace, a wounded state.

This "anti-history" has persisted for decades, requiring enormous efforts to challenge. I can attest to this personally. During the first half of the 1950s, I studied at the Faculty of Philosophy and Literature at the University of Madrid, graduating in history and in Semitic philology. As my memory serves me, nobody within the faculty during my time there made the slightest reference to the Palestinian question. Although the history curriculum included courses on the contemporary era and the "History of Contemporary Islam" was offered as a course, it too omitted any study of Palestine. The study plan for the same syllabus included another subject, the generically termed, "History of the Israeli People." But again, no reference was made to the events of 1948: the founding of the Israeli State on Palestinian land.

It was only when I traveled to Cairo between 1957 and 1962 that I began to hear of Palestine and its people, after which I traveled with my wife to Palestinian lands, which at that time were part of the Hashemite Kingdom of Jordan. This marked the beginning of my commitment to Palestine, to which I remain fiercely committed intellectually and personally, many years later.

In 1967, I began working with my good friend, the Palestinian poet Mahmud Sobh, who had arrived in Madrid from Damascus to complete his PhD, examining an extensive anthology of contemporary Palestinian poetry titled "The Resistance." The revelatory book on the subject by Ghassan Kanafani, in Arabic, and other work by other authors in the same linguistic area had just been published. Our anthology was the first European-language book on the subject. Once we'd completed the book, we began looking for a publisher. Several publishing houses would tell us they'd "misplaced" the manuscript, but it was thanks, in 1969, to the help of an institution created at that time by a patron of Tunisian origin, Casa Hispano-Árabe, that we were able to publish the work.

All of this goes to illustrate a long-term phenomenon: the amelioration not only of the "Palestinian question," in particular, but recognition of Palestine per se. The Palestinian question has been intentionally robbed of origins, of roots, rendering us unable to make sense of history. The history of the Palestinian question is replete with outrages against the truth and crimes against memory, truly "plagued" with crimes against humanity.

And all of this underscores one of this book's main virtues: it radically confronts, with integrity, so much of the intentionally distorted, false, or simply ignorant historiography on the subject. It focuses precisely on salvaging and bringing to light many of the roots, the origins, of the Palestinian question.

In this book, we encounter "the before times"; a history kept buried, banished, just as the Palestinians were banished from their land, covering the period between the last decades of the nineteenth century and the middle of the twentieth century. It begs the question: is there anything more cruel than the denial of time? This book allows us to visually encounter the idea that time can be recovered and a history that should not have been banished.

This exceptional photo album, this incredibly rich set of images, is profoundly original, of *origin*. It provides testimony to the imaginary as a collection of moments, situations in which the viewer encounters the unknown, the unexpected, and often the surprising.

An image is always, by itself, a valuable object, but its value increases if not reduced strictly to the physical gaze, a "seeing," which is also subjective and sensitive. With this triple gaze, the contemplated object acquires all its richness, value, and meaning. This magnificent collection of images takes form in this triple way of vision: eyes, mind, and feeling unified in the gaze; the seeing is integral.

The people in these images inhabited a country by no means extensive, a little more than 20,000 km,^{2} with a population of over a million in 1948. This population, limited as it was in number and space, was surprisingly diverse in its expressions, its behaviors, in its habits, customs, and ways of existing, suffering, and thriving. Did Palestine, at once singular and plural, unique and multidimensional, deserve to be destroyed, deformed, replaced? Did these people not deserve to continue living as these images reveal that they lived? We confront this question in the eyes staring back at us, haunting us as we turn the pages of this book.

The texts in this book, written by experts on the Palestinian question, are complementary to each other, with each of the authors contributing personal and professional experience. Bichara Khader is a Palestinian living in exile abroad; Johnny Mansour is a Palestinian living in Palestine, and therefore in internal exile; and Teresa Aranguren is Spanish with a deep connection to Palestine. I've been fortunate to enjoy an unbreakable friendship with Teresa and Bichara, as I've been lucky to maintain an unbreakable bond with Palestine and its people. Writing these pages has not only allowed me to express my solidarity and admiration for them, but also allowed me to discover the work of Sandra Barrilaro, whose sensitivity and experience in working with photographic material has been fundamental in the selection of these images.

When writing or speaking about Palestine, I often refer to the words of one of the most important Palestinian writers of our time, Rashad Abu-Shawir: "The Palestinian question is not just a problem of borders (*hudud*), but a problem of existence (*wujud*)." It is not that the Palestinian people exist, but that they existed, and they will continue to exist. And that existence requires not only a home, but a homeland, a state: Palestine. Dirty politics cannot bend the clean reality of existence, nor can it ultimately deny or marginalize it. Existence is not a mask, nor can it be masked, and to deny existence is to deny life: it is a crime. A crime that persists without judge, jury, or sentence. This is what these photos recall and affirm.

Pedro Martínez Montávez,
Professor Emeritus,
Autonomous University of Madrid

xiv

Palestine: The Hidden Question

Before Palestine became a name synonymous with conflict, or indeed one antonymous to the existence of the State of Israel, it was simply Palestine. Obvious as this may be, it is often forgotten. And that forgetting did not happen by chance. The name Palestine, which appeared in Egyptian inscriptions in the twelfth century BC, is the name that over the centuries has been designated in geographical, historical, cultural, sociological, demographic, administrative, and political terms to the area. Between the Mediterranean and the Jordan, between the mountains north of Galilee and the Sinai Desert, the territory that in the Roman Empire was called Palestine is identified with that which in the nineteenth century, with the same name, was part of the Syrian province of the Ottoman Empire. A land as old as the history of mankind, replete with religious and historical connotations for East and West, Palestine above all is the land in which the Palestinians lived.

The Arab–Israeli conflict is ancient but not ancestral. It does not sink into the depths of time, nor is it inscribed in the genes of its people; it has a date and place of birth. At the end of the nineteenth century, the lives and collective destinies of the peoples of this region were thrown into disarray, as Palestine became the "Palestinian question." The Zionist project that began to take shape in official European circles not only generated an uncertain future for the Arab population of Palestine but would also end up redrawing its past as the prelude to the future Jewish state.

The first Zionist settlers arrived on Palestinian land in the 1880s when the region was still under Ottoman rule, settling in the fertile coastal plain north of Jaffa on land acquired by Baron Edmond Rothschild, a key figure in financing and advancing the movement. Many of these purchases were made by taking advantage of the 1876 land legislation that allowed the Ottoman administration and some large landowners in Istanbul and Beirut to conduct profitable business, seizing the lands of notable Palestinians who could not afford the punishing taxes levied by the Ottoman Empire, which were then

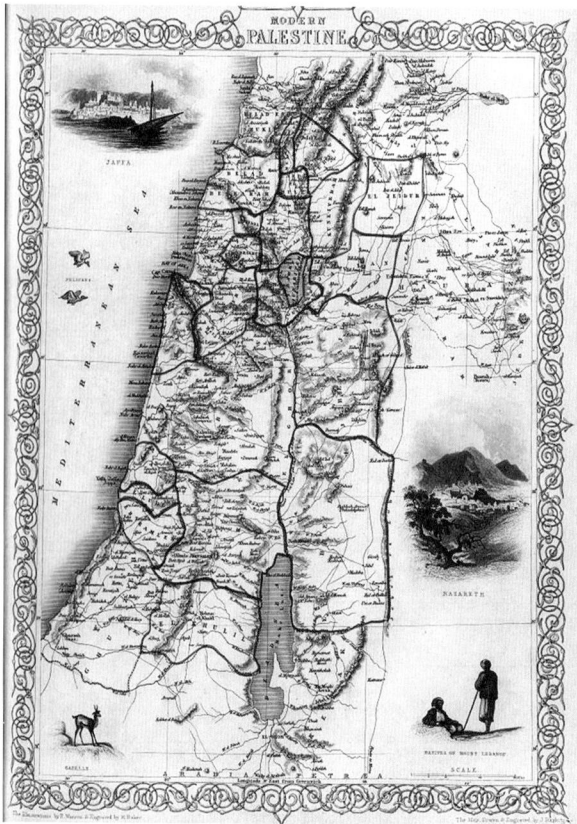

Modern Palestine, 1851, by John Rapkin. From J. Rapkin, London and New York, J. & F. Tallis

resold later at the disproportionately high prices that the likes of Rothschild and the Palestine Jewish Colonization Association (PICA) were able to pay.

At that time the arrival of Europeans settlers to the Holy Land was not uncommon. From the middle of the century, groups of devout Christians and Jews had emigrated to Palestine for religious reasons. The German colonists from the Society of Templars who established themselves in Haifa, Jaffa, Jerusalem, and other towns in the area, or the Swedish and North American families who settled in a beautiful building in Jerusalem—now the American Colony Hotel—are some examples of the imprint that flow of religious emigrants left in the region.

Palestine was by no means closed to foreigners, nor was it a hostile or religiously fanatical society when the first Zionist settlers arrived there. And contrary to the propaganda that endures, the land which they settled was neither empty nor in fact a desert.

This is how two Spanish travelers, José María Fernández Sánchez and Francisco Freire Ferreiro, described the Jaffa region in 1875:

> There are extensive forests of pomegranate, orange, lemon, apple, sugarcane and palm. Its beautiful gardens have a great variety of plants, orchards with all kinds of legumes and vegetables, all nourished with water drawn by a multitude of waterwheels. Nature is prodigious…It has some extraordinary gardens that provide possibly the first oranges in the world…These are the best orange groves in the world.[*]

In 1891, the Russian Jewish writer Asher Ginsberg, who wrote under the pen name Ehad Ha'am, described a visit he made to Palestine:

> From abroad, we are accustomed to believe that Eretz Israel is presently almost totally desolate, an unculti-

---

[*] José María Fernández Sánchez and Francisco Freire Barreiro, *Santiago, Jerusalem, Rome. Diary of a Pilgrimage to These and Other Holy Places*, 1882, cited in Pedro Martínez Montávez, *Pensando en la historia de los árabes* (Madrid: Cantarabia, 1995).

vated desert, and that anyone wishing to buy land there can come and buy all he wants. But in truth, it is not so. In the entire land, it is hard to find tillable land that is not already tilled: only sandy fields and stony hills, suitable at best for planting trees or vine.[*]

Palestine was not a desert waiting for the arrival of foreign settlers to make it flourish. As with other regions of the Mediterranean basin, it had areas of desert and areas which were arable, some of which were very richly fertile and laboriously cultivated by farmers who had settled there for generations.

In reality, the Zionist colonies by themselves did not generate profit, and their subsistence depended on the capital of the Rothschilds and later on the Jewish National Fund. But unlike the local farmers, who were almost always in debt, the new settlers had a sort of bad credit that didn't require repayment. This is reflected in a report on the distribution of land in Palestine, commissioned by the British government from Sir John Hope Simpson in 1930: "Of the agricultural settlements it may be said that none of the Zionist settlements are self-supporting in the sense that they would be able to maintain themselves without further assistance"[†]

From the second half of the nineteenth century, land in Palestine changed hands with relative frequency, while those who worked it remained there. This changed radically with the arrival of the first Zionist colonists. Those families who for generations had sharecropping or lease arrangements now cultivated land acquired by the multimillionaire Rothschild or by the Jewish National Fund and were expelled from their homes and farms. This was exacerbated by the policy of Judaization, which would become a priority of the Zionist movement.

A Jewish National Fund contract established the following:

> The tenant agrees to perform any work related to the cultivation of the property using exclusively Jewish labor … the contract also provides that the land may not be granted to a non-Jewish person. If the landholder dies and leaves a non-Jewish heir, the Fund will avail itself of the right of restitution…[‡]

For the Zionist movement, the acquisition of land was not enough. The land had to be free of its people.

---

[*] Ehad Ha'am, "Truth from Eretz Israel," translated by Alan Dowty, *Israel Studies* 5, no. 2 (Fall 2000): xx.
[†] Sir John Hope Simpson, *Report on Immigration, Land Settlement and Development in Palestine*, 1930.
[‡] Simpson, *Report on Immigration*.

~The Great War~

In the years before World War I, the eastern Arab world was immersed in nationalist political turmoil in the face of Ottoman rule. In Palestine, the reinvigorated national question was supported by protests by dispossessed peasants who accused the Ottoman administration of passivity against the Zionist advance. In an interview in the daily *Al-lqdam* in March 1914, Palestinian intellectual Khalil al-Sakakini observed:

> In the months prior to the outbreak of the war, newspapers such as Falastín, Al Karmel and Al-Iqdam launched a campaign denouncing Zionism: "The Zionists want to take over Palestine, that is, the heart of the Arab countries ... If you want to kill cut off a nation's tongue and occupy its territory; this is what the Zionists intend to do with the Arab nation."*

The Great War spelled the end of the Ottoman Empire and ushered Great Britain and France onto the scene. Throughout 1915 and 1916, the British High Commissioner in Egypt, Sir Henry McMahon, and Sheriff Hussein of Mecca exchanged a series of letters in which the British government pledged recognition and support for the independence of the Syrian provinces under Ottoman rule in exchange for Hussein declaring war against the Ottomans. The Arabs fought on the side of the Allies, confident that, once the conflict was over, they would gain independence. But while McMahon was making this commitment to Hussein, the British government secretly negotiated with his French counterpart the division of the Arab territories of the Ottoman Empire. The agreement, named after the diplomats who signed it, Sykes and Picot, awarded France the territory of present-day Syria and Lebanon; Britain was given control over Iraq, Transjordan (present-day Jordan), and Palestine. The dramatic fate of the Palestinian people was being redrawn in government offices in London.

In a letter of November 1917 to Baron Lionel Walter Rothschild, Sir Arthur James Balfour, Her Majesty's Foreign Minister, pledged Great Britain's support for the creation of a National Home for the Jewish People in Palestine. The famous Balfour Declaration was in principle a simple confidential letter with no legal validity. But legality meant nothing when it came to colonial interests. An illustration of this imperialist cynicism is found in the following paragraph of a memorandum written by Lord Balfour to his government in 1919:

---

* Khalil al-Sakakini, who hailed from a prominent Palestinian Christian family, was one of the founders of the Jerusalem Constitutional School and a leading figure, like many other Christian intellectuals, of the Arab National Movement.

We do not propose even to go through the form of consulting the wishes of the present inhabitants of the country… The four Great Powers are committed to Zionism. And Zionism, be it right or wrong, good or bad, is rooted in age-long traditions, in present needs, in future hopes, of far profounder import than the desires and prejudices of the 700,000 Arabs who now inhabit that ancient land.[*]

On December 9, 1917, following the surrender of Ottoman troops, the British Army entered Jerusalem, led by General Allenby. Palestine remained under British military control until July 1922, when the League of Nations established the British Mandate on Palestine, which included the commitment to the Balfour Declaration, that is, to the creation of a National Home for the Jewish People in Palestine.

According to the 1921 census carried out by the British administration, the population of Palestine was 762,000, of which 76.9 percent were Muslim, 11.6 percent Christian, 10.6 percent Jewish, and 0.9 percent of other denominations. As for land ownership, only 2.4 percent of the total land area of the country was in the hands of the Zionist movement.

While it was evident that the British administration was aligned with the objectives of Zionism, the leaders and the cultural elite of Palestinian society still hoped the London government would heed their claims and cease its policy of collaboration with the Zionists. Committees, commissions, and delegations were organized that traveled to England again and again to present their arguments, provide accounts of the unrest within the population, and warn of potential outbreaks of violence. In a letter sent in 1921 to the then Secretary of State for the Colonies, Sir Winston Churchill, the Arab Congress described the situation as follows:

The very serious and growing unrest among the Palestinians arises from their absolute conviction that the present policy of the British Government is directed towards evicting them from their country in order to make it a national state for immigrant Jews…The Balfour Declaration was made without our being consulted and we cannot accept it as deciding our destinies.[†]

The breaking point came in August 1929. Following a Jewish-led demonstration that culminated in the raising of

---

* Sir Arthur James Balfour, Documents on British Foreign Policy 1919–1939.
† Letter to Churchill from the Arab Delegation that traveled to London to oppose the inclusion of the Balfour Declaration in the terms of the British Mandate for Palestine, October 24, 1921.

the Zionist flag at the Wailing Wall, a large number of Jerusalem's Muslims took to the streets, and the protests spread throughout the territory and resulted in assaults on the Jewish neighborhoods of Hebron, Safad, and Tel Aviv. By the end of the riots, 133 Jews and 116 Arabs had been killed, with almost 1,000 detainees and 26 (25 Arabs and 1 Jew) sentenced to death for their part in the events.

⌒ The Great Revolt ⌒

Anti-British and anti-Zionist agitation reached all parts of Palestinian society. Women were also heavily mobilized: the First Palestine Arab Women's Congress took place in 1932, and delegations of Muslim and Christian women met with Mandate authorities and traveled to London to present the demands of the national movement.

By the mid-1930s, the climate was one of all-out rebellion. In May 1936, the Arab Higher Committee chaired by Haj Amin Al-Husseini launched a call for civil disobedience and called a general strike throughout the territory. The great Palestinian revolt had begun: the first intifada.

The strike, which paralyzed economic and commercial activity in the country, lasted six months; the revolt lasted three years. British repression took a brutal toll: more than 1,000 Palestinians were killed, 2,500 arrested, and 54 sentenced to death by hanging. But it seemed that some political gains had been made. In May 1939, the British government published a White Paper announcing restrictions on Jewish immigration and a commitment to granting independence to Palestine within ten years. For the Zionist movement, this turn in British politics seriously jeopardized its project of a Jewish state.

Despite the rapid acceleration of immigration and land acquisition in this period, the Zionist leaders were well aware that their goals of obtaining more land and of becoming a majority would only be possible through force.

The director of the Jewish National Fund, Yosef Weitz, expressed this clearly in 1940:

> There is no way besides transferring the Arabs from here to the neighboring countries, to transfer them all; except maybe for Bethlehem, Nazareth and Old Jerusalem. We must not leave a single village, not a single tribe. And the transfer must be directed to Iraq, to Syria, and even to Transjordan . . . And only with such a

transfer will the country be able to absorb millions of our brothers, and the Jewish question shall be solved.*

At the same time, a bloody war was being waged in Europe, with England and the allied countries devoting all their energies to the fight against Nazi Germany. The fate of the Palestinian population was the least of the British government's concerns. The promises reflected in the White Paper were never going to be fulfilled.

Following the presentation of the White Paper, which did meet some of the Palestinian demands, the most extreme sectors of Zionism declared war against the Mandate authorities and unleashed a wave of terrorist actions. In July 1946, Irgun Zvai Leumi, an armed Zionist group, detonated a bomb in the King David Hotel, headquarters of the British administration, killing ninety-one officials. Six months later, Britain revoked the Mandate for Palestine, delegating its responsibilities to the United Nations.

In November 1947, the United Nations General Assembly adopted the Partition Plan for Palestine, establishing two states for two peoples, one Arab and the other Jewish. Great Britain abstained from voting. The plan granted 57 percent of the territory to the future Jewish state and 43 percent to the Arab state.

The population of Palestine at that time was 1,972,000, of whom 608,000, a third, were Jewish. About 47.7 percent of the lands were classified as Arab property, 6.6 percent Jewish property, and the remaining 46 percent were communal and public lands.†

The establishment of the Jewish state would not have been possible without ridding the territory of its Arab population.

Teresa Aranguren, Journalist

---

* Yosef Weitz, Diary, 1940, cited in Ilan Halevi, *Sous Israël, la Palestine* (Paris: Le Sycomore, 1978), xx.
† Proceedings of the United Nations ad hoc Commission for Palestine.

The Palestinian Nakba (1947–1949): A Sociocide

Between 1917 and 1947, Palestine was held completely hostage to the maneuvers of British colonialism. In the 1917 Balfour Declaration, Great Britain promised the Zionist movement a Jewish National Home in Palestine. At that time, Jews represented 6 percent of the population and owned barely 1 percent of the land.

During the twenty-six-year period of the British Mandate (1922–1948), successive waves of Zionist immigrants transformed the demographic composition of Palestine, and by 1947, Jews formed 33 percent of the total population but still owned only 6.6 percent of the territory. British support of the Zionist movement was assured—a support, it must be stated, not driven by philanthropic motives. The postwar Middle East produced a consensus between the Zionist objective of colonizing Palestine and the British objective of securing a base of support in the vicinity of the Suez Canal. The Zionist project served the interests of British imperial strategy.

However disastrous the role played by the British would prove for the Palestinian people, it should not obscure the role of the Zionist movement, which, since its first congress in Basel in 1897, had decided to establish a Jewish state in Palestine—which clearly and emphatically meant the "de-Arabization" of Palestine or, in other words, the "invisibilization" of its people to facilitate the Judaization of the country.

The early twentieth century propaganda slogan "a land without a people for a people without a land" represents the hard nucleus of Zionist ideology. Chaim Weizmann, one of the movement's leaders, candidly acknowledged the Zionist texts as containing almost no mention of the Arabs.

But the Palestinians did exist, and they lived in their land and defended it, as demonstrated by the numerous revolts against the British politics of complicity with the Zionist project that marked the years of the Mandate between the two world wars. Indeed, Ben-Gurion, the future president of Israel, made this revealing statement: "Let us not ignore the truth among ourselves … politically we are the aggressors and they defend themselves… The country is theirs, because they inhabit it, whereas we want to come here and settle down, and in their view we want to take away from them their country."*

Not limited solely to establishing itself on Palestinian land, the Zionist movement required the uprooting of the Palestinian people. As such, various means—symbolic, institutional, and financial—were used to exert control, manifested through colonial and exclusive concepts such as the "inalienability" of the lands conquered by the Jews and the prohibition of Palestinian peasants (Christians and Muslims) from continuing to work on those lands.

During World War II, the Zionist movement was already firmly established in Palestine, but its leaders were aware that the role of the British was coming to an end, and thus began to transfer the mechanisms of the pro-Zionist lobby to the United States. The perception of British patronage had begun to shift; they were now viewed as a roadblock in the path to Jewish statehood. In the mid-1940s, armed Zionist groups such as the Stern, the Irgun, and the Palmach launched a wave of terrorist acts against the Palestinians and the British. On July 22, 1946, an attack on the headquarters of the British army in Jerusalem, the King David Hotel, was carried out by the Jewish terrorist group Irgun Zvai Leumi, causing more than ninety deaths.

Despite the costly presence of almost 100,000 British troops (one soldier for every eighteen Palestinians), the Mandate authorities were unable to keep a handle on the situation. On February 18, 1947, the British threw in the towel, with Ernest Bevin, Secretary of State for Foreign Affairs, announcing to Parliament, "we have decided to ask the United Nations for a solution," while British public opinion demanded the end of the campaign with the slogan "bring the boys home." On April 28, 1947, a special session of the UN General Assembly was convened at Flushing Meadows to consider the British government's request to bring an end to the Mandate.

---

* David Ben-Gurion. Appearing in Simha Flapan, *Zionism and the Palestinians* (Ann Arbor: University of Michigan Press, 1979), 141–42, citing a 1938 speech.

~Sociocide~

In 1947, the British took the Palestinian question to the UN. Various commissions were created, working groups were formed, successive plans were drawn up and others were rejected: a provincial autonomy plan, a federal plan, a confederate plan, and others. Finally, on September 23, 1947, the UN General Assembly created an ad hoc commission to make definitive proposals. Two proposals were presented: one, the partition of Palestine into two states; another, a single federal state. The Zionists opposed the federal plan in favor of a Jewish rather than binational state. With 33 votes in favor, 13 against, and 10 abstentions or absences, this was the Partition Plan adopted by the General Assembly. The United States used all possible means, including financial pressure, diplomatic intimidation, and even threats to Latin American countries, to garner support for the Partition Plan.*

The Zionists greeted the resolution with glee, the Palestinians with fear and bewilderment. The resolution divided Palestine into six main regions: three of them (56.0 percent of the total area) were to form the Jewish state, and the other three (43.35 percent) were to form the Palestinian state, while Jerusalem and its surroundings (0.65 percent) would become an international zone.

The UN arrangement meant that the Jews, who represented 33 percent of the population and owned only 6 percent of the total area, were granted 56 percent of the territory. This primordial injustice would be immediately compounded by ethnic cleansing carried out by the armed Zionist groups, a process intimately linked to the project of a "predominantly Jewish state." While the territory designated for the Palestinian state was fairly demographically homogeneous (725,000 Arabs and 10,000 Jews), the territory allotted to the Jewish state comprised 272 Arab villages, 183 Jewish villages, and a near-equivalent population of 509,780 Arabs and 499,000 Jews.† The partition plan planted the seeds of the Palestinian catastrophe.

Following the passage of the UN resolution on November 29, 1947, the Zionist leaders launched a systematic campaign of ethnic cleansing. The objective was to conquer "the maximum territory with the minimum population." On March 10, 1948, the Zionist leadership led by Ben-Gurion gave the green light to the so-called Plan Dalet, which established

---

* See my published works: Bichara Khader, *Histoire de la Palestine*, 3 volumes, *Maison Tunisienne de L'Édition, 1975-1976*; and *Los hijos de Agenor, Europa y Palestina desde las Cruzadas hasta el siglo xxi* (Barcelona: Ediciones Bellaterra, 2000).

† From the United Nations Partition Plan for Palestine: On 29 November 1947, the UN General Assembly adopted the Plan as Resolution 181.

the military strategy to rid the territory of its Arab population. In his book *The Ethnic Cleansing of Palestine*, Israeli historian Ilan Pappé describes part of this master plan:

> These operations can be carried out in the following manner: either by destroying villages (by setting fire to them, by blowing them up, and by planting mines in their debris) and especially of those population centers which are difficult to control continuously; or by mounting combing and control operations according to the following guidelines: encirclement of the villages, conducting a search inside them. In case of resistance, the armed forces must be wiped out and the population expelled outside the borders of the state.[*]

Palestine now faced its worst catastrophe: the forced exile of two thirds of its Arab population. Palestinian historian Saleh Abdel Jawad describes this as a form of "sociocide," signifying "the total destruction of the Palestinians, not only as a political entity or national political group but as a people."

The plan consisted of attacking Palestinian villages, massacring part of their population, and forcing the rest into permanent exile without any possibility of return. Israeli historian Benny Morris puts it bluntly: "For most of 1948, ideas about how to consolidate and eternalize the Palestinian exile began to crystallize, and the destruction of villages was immediately perceived as a primary means of achieving this goal."[†]

Palestinian scholar and writer Walid Khalidi puts the figure at 418 Palestinian towns destroyed in the months before and after the creation of the State of Israel, while other sources estimate the number of Palestinian villages destroyed or transformed into *kibbutzim, nahalim, or moshavim* at 531. Between December 1947 and June 1948, almost two-thirds of the Palestinian people (731,000) were forcibly exiled.

Perhaps the most symbolic event in this campaign of terror is the massacre of Deir Yassin. This village on the outskirts of Jerusalem was attacked by Irgun troops on April 9, 1948. The Red Cross delegate in Jerusalem, Jacques de Reynier, was one of the first witnesses to arrive at the scene. He recounts it as follows: "Three hundred persons were massacred … without any military reason or provocation of any kind; old men, women, children, newly-born were savagely murdered

---

[*] Ilan Pappé, *The Ethnic Cleansing of Palestine* (London: One World, 2006).
[†] Benny Morris, *The Birth of the Palestinian Refugee Problem, 1947–1949* (Cambridge: Cambridge Middle East Library, 1987).

with grenades and knives by Jewish troops of the Irgun, entirely under the control of their chiefs."*

Menachem Begin, Irgun leader and thus the person responsible for the massacre, noted in his memoir, *The Revolt*: "Without the victory in Deir Yasin, the State of Israel would not have existed."† In other words, without the Palestinian exodus, without ethnic cleansing, Israel would not have seen the light of day as a Jewish state. In fact, before the proclamation of the State of Israel and the outbreak of the first Arab–Israeli war, almost 300,000 Palestinians had already been forced into exile. This contradicts one of the key tenets of Israeli propaganda, attributing to the war declared by the Arab states on Israel the responsibility for the flight of Palestinian refugees.

On the afternoon of May 14, 1948, Sir Alan Cunningham, the seventh and last of the British High Commissioners in Palestine, boarded the HMS Euryalus. It was the end of the British Mandate in Palestine. The next day, May 15, 1948, Ben-Gurion proclaimed the birth of the State of Israel. And exactly eleven minutes later, the United States recognized the provisional government headed by David Ben-Gurion as the de facto authority of the newly created state.

Under pressure from their peoples, the Arab states made efforts to derail the Zionist project, but Israel continued to expand its borders through forced land evacuation and the uprooting of Palestinian communities. This was "planned sociocide," the systematic destruction of an entire people. Indeed, Israeli leaders, including Ben-Gurion, referred to ethnic cleansing with the euphemism of "forced transfer." As early as 1940, Joseph Weitz, director of the Land and Afforestation Department, declared: "We must not leave a single village, not a single tribe."‡

In her book *Palestine: History of a Conflict*, Clara M. Thomas de Antonio cites a 2003 documentary, *Route 181*, in which a seventy-three-year-old Israeli Jew proudly recounts the exploits of his youth as part of Operation Matateh, or "Operation Broom," in 1948: "We kicked them out of the region to create a Jewish territorial continuity. We formed a chain. We were well-armed, obviously. We were the Iftah regiment, a battalion of 1,500 men … we chased them. We were advancing by driving them towards Jordan. To a region from which they could not return."§ In *Palestine: The Thread of Memory*, Teresa Aranguren provides the testimony of a refugee who described the massacre of Tantura, a village located in the coastal area south of Haifa: "The people of Tantura were stubborn, refusing to leave their village … when the Jewish

* Jacques de Reynier, *À Jerusalem un drapeau flottait sur la ligne de feu* (Paris: Ed. de la Braconnière, 1950).
† Menachem Begin, *The Revolt* (London: W.A. Allen, 1951).
‡ See Noam Chomsky, *Fateful Triangle: The United States, Israel, and the Palestinians.* Updated Edition (Chicago: Haymarket Books, 1999), 131.
§ Clara. M. Thomas de Antonio, *Palestina, Historia de un conflicto* (Sevilla: Universidad de Sevilla, 2006).

soldiers entered the village, they separated the women and children and sent them in trucks to Tulkarem. The men were divided into groups, placed in different parts of the town, and machine-gunned down."* All of this disproves Israeli propaganda that the Palestinians simply fled combat zones, shedding a different light on the famous Zionist slogan, widely repeated from 1948 to the present day, that the Israeli army is the most "moral" of armies.

The destruction of Palestinian society was a strategic undertaking. A "sociocide" accompanied by a "memoricide," as the former Israeli minister of defense Moshe Dayan acknowledged in an address to a Haifa University audience: "Jewish villages were built in the place of Arab villages … There is not a single place built in this country that did not have a former Arab population."†

Alarmed by the atrocity of the events and by the risk that this could lead to a broader regional uprising, the United States and France proposed that the UN send a mediator to Palestine in charge of seeking a peaceful way out of the Palestinian quagmire. Count Bernadotte, nephew of the King of Sweden, was placed in charge of this mediation. In the report that Bernadotte finished writing on the night of September 15–16, 1948, he stated: "There have been numerous reports from reliable sources of large-scale looting, pillaging, and plundering, and of instances of destruction of villages without apparent military necessity. The liability of the Provisional Government of Israel to restore private property to its Arab owners and to indemnify those owners for property wantonly destroyed is clear."‡

In the report, Bernadotte made the following suggestions: the addition of Western Galilee to the Jewish state, the Negev to the Arab state, the West Bank to Transjordan, the internationalization of Jerusalem, and "the return of Palestinian refugees to their homes." This last suggestion was, of course, inadmissible for the authorities of the newly created State of Israel, which was designed to be ethnically Jewish. On September 17, 1948—that is, the day after he filed his report—Bernadotte and his companion French Colonel Andre Serot were assassinated by the Jewish terrorist Stern Gang.

On December 11, 1948, the General Assembly of the United Nations adopted resolution 194. Article 11 states: "refugees wishing to return to their homes and live at peace with their neighbors should be permitted to do so at the earliest practicable date, and . . . compensation should be paid for the property of those choosing not to return and for loss of or

---

* Teresa Aranguren, *Palestina: el hilo de la memoria* (Barcelona: Barataria, 2012).
† Moshe Dayan, address to the Technion, Haifa, reported in Haaretz, April 4, 1969.
‡ Count Folke Bernadotte, UN Mediator on Palestine, Progress Report, September 1948.

damage to property which, under principles of international law or equity, should be made good by the Governments or authorities responsible."

This resolution, like many others, was made in vain. It did not prevent Bernadotte's successor, Dr. Bunche, from presiding over the signature of armistice agreements between Israel and Egypt on February 24, 1949, followed by other agreements with Lebanon on March 23, with Jordan on April 3, and with Syria on July 20. The Arab states undersigned their political and military defeat. At the end of 1949, Israel controlled 78 percent of the territory of Palestine. The Palestinian people were dispersed into exile or to refugee camps in the West Bank, Gaza, Jordan, Lebanon, and Syria.

In December 1949, the number of Palestinian refugees officially registered by the United Nations reached 940,000. That same year, the UN created the United Nations Relief and Works Agency (UNRWA), a special agency tasked with provision of food, healthcare, and education for Palestinian refugees. The agency was originally intended to be provisional, "until the refugees can return to their homes."*

To this day, the Palestinian tragedy remains an open wound. Thanks to the shameful indifference of the West and the international community, the Nakba of 1948 has become a permanent Nakba.

Bichara Khader, professor,
University of Louvain, Belgium

---

* Cited in Ghada Hashem Talhami, *Palestinian Refugees: Pawns to Political Actors* (New York, Nova Publishers, 2003), 194.

Photography as Historical Text for Reinforcing Survival

My story has always been that of Palestine—whether in house and home, with my parents having been forced to flee, experiencing all the hardships the Palestinian people were made to endure in 1948, and later, when I lived in Wadi al-Nasnas, one of the poorest and most marginalized neighborhoods in Haifa. Or in secondary school when my true sense of national identity was forming at the same time as the Palestinian cause was taking on new dimensions.

My Palestine has been drawn not just from family memories passed down through the generations, but also through my search for new ways of discovering and telling its history. In the period between high school and college, I began gathering oral histories of elders from Haifa, Acre ('Akka), Shafa 'Amr, Nazareth, and the towns of Galilee (al-Jalil). Those I interviewed told me about their lives before the disaster, the Nakba of 1948, when they lived in better circumstances, albeit under the British Mandate. Some would show me photos from that time, personal snapshots of family and private life as well as photos of public life, of their communities. Others would pull out property and land deeds, documents of sites zealously plundered by Zionist settlers.

As questions were swirling in my head around oral history as a means to connect people to their place of birth, around how these people contributed to Palestinian society, and how to transfer this history to younger generations, I encountered an ever-growing number of photos during my visits. Many were eager to bring out their photo albums, and we'd turn the pages discovering family histories, their relationships with the places they'd lived, and always their ceaseless, permanent longing for those days. Quite a few gave me original photos, which I incorporated into articles and historical research, published in books and local newspapers, and presented at conferences organized throughout Palestine, which in turn encouraged others to take another look at the contents of their own family albums.

The function and interplay of oral history and photography as historical narrative and (subsequently) Palestinian historical narrative are worth examining. My own narrative is that of my people, who have been subject for over a hundred years to every kind of forced expulsion, expatriation, and cultural extermination, all for the establishment of a state for a people unconnected to one another, brought together by the Zionist movement in absolute complicity and accordance with the colonial system.

Oral history in the Palestinian context allows us to mark our existence within place, from places from which we were expelled. Oral history tells the Palestinian story, laden as it is with images from the past, opening up pathways of research. It is people's history, accessible through its freedom of expression and freedom from the rigidity of academic historical writing and historiography. Through oral history, we can identify and define a space and return to it through the Palestinian subject, alive in the realities, sensations, and images of the past that have never left us as Palestinians, and act intensely in shaping our individual and collective historical memory.

What gives strength to this history is that which remains in the Palestinian memory—the details, facts, private and collective, about daily life. And this is reinforced by photographs and those documents that have been preserved despite the displacement of their owners. The intense relationship between time, space, and photography provides, I believe, the most qualified testimony of what takes place on the stage of history. It is precisely the form of a still image that conveys details of changes over time, providing the viewer the opportunity to go back in time, to the time and place where it was taken. The collection of testimony and oral history allows for the rooting of Palestine's existence within the Palestinian place. Because of this, I believe that Palestinian oral history should not be confined to the framework of "past" history, since it is appropriate to orient it and extract from it something that is implicit within it: a sense of the future that offers a strong possibility of returning. And that return is possible.

The concept of the Palestinian right of return, in this context, is a strategic historical process that allows the future to become present. The spatio-temporal or chrono-spatial relationship of an image does not reflect simply the reality of what was, but rather, Palestinian oral history allows us to reconstruct that which links Palestinians to place and time. And that space changed; for the Palestinians of the diaspora and for refugees, time froze the moment they were forced to flee, bringing with them the image of their place and their community in that moment. As that temporal image is no longer what it was, a nostalgic imaginary reclaiming allows us to keep that spatial heritage as something untouchable, offering visual pathways where meaning is perceptible to the viewer, while in reality the place itself has become unrecognizable.

The photographic image, in harmonizing time and space, behaves semiotically, revealing a certain, unrepeatable reality, of people and characteristics that are in the image, the symbols of that image understood (or perhaps not) by the viewer. It carries with it and expresses messages both explicit and implicit, seen in their own way, inviting us to go back—to remember. And for those aware of what appears in the photo, it is a reinforcement of knowledge and memory. While the form is inherently static, it allows us to interact with the time–space axis by virtue of collective and individual memory.

In working with various historical materials—texts (personal and public documents and papers), photographs, and Palestinian oral history—I've paid special attention to my hometown, Haifa, where I've always lived, and whose people were forcibly and savagely expatriated in 1948, such that of its original 75,000 Palestinian inhabitants only 3,000 remained. The refusal by the official Israeli governmental and municipal institutions to take responsibility for the Nakba they caused, in both Haifa and across Palestine, is nothing short of barbarism.

Over time, and through what has ultimately become an enormous accumulation of photographs of the city and documents, I have been able to systematically publish, in a series of exhibitions, the photographs I gathered from family albums, archives, and other sources. Each exhibition allows me to observe the movement and behavior of the spectators, their interaction with the images, and their verbal responses, their thoughts. The historical accounts of the Palestinian people, through text and through photography, reflect for us the magnificence and beauty of a dynamic society that worked to build itself intellectually, socially, economically, and culturally from an agrarian to an increasingly urban society. Most of the photos were taken in cities, in which there were quite a few photography studios and field photographers, and where many families owned their own cameras, more so than in smaller towns and villages.

I firmly believe that while the people of Palestine lost their land, they refuse to lose their history. As one of the children, the survivors, of this people, I know how sincere our relationship is with the land, its past, its history, its images, its documents. Taken together, they return to us what we need the most: our homeland.

Johnny Mansour, professor and historian based in Haifa.

About the Selection of Photographs: Exposing Palestine

"Every photograph is a certificate of presence."

Roland Barthes, *Camera Lucida: Reflections on Photography*

As long as the occupation continues to produce refugees, we must continue to remember. Because memories cannot be colonized or exiled and because there is power in evocation, for as Palestinian poet Mahmoud Darwish reminds us, we know the invaders' fear of memories.*

All while familiar with magnificent pre-1948 photo collections such as Walid Khalidi's *Before Their Diaspora*, or the work of the erudite Elias Sanbar, *The Palestinians,* I decided, along with the journalist Teresa Aranguren, to add a grain of sand to the living memory of a people; to the Palestine that existed before the catastrophe, the Nakba. We must keep remembering, giving new light to images drawn with light and making public photographs taken within the private sphere, of families and friendships that sat together in cafés, at a time when the fabric of society was woven in another way. Photographs taken at a time when the banalization of the image was less ubiquitous.

In these photographs, time and tragedy provide another layer of meaning. The snapshots that we would discover filled us with wonder, admiration, tenderness, anger—for a lost world, for a people expelled from their lives and their lands. A society rocked by the trauma of expulsion, never to be the same again. Photographs which reveal the innocence of everyday gestures, of a people unaware of their fate. Images that serve as a reminder of the human condition of a society that cannot be erased. Portraits that bring us closer to ourselves, our ancestors, and that bring us back to our own family albums.

We began a search for photos that hadn't been previously published, with the intention of enhancing that memory. This wasn't an easy task given that in the first half of the twentieth century, most families didn't have access to a camera,

---

* See Darwish's "On This Earth," reprinted in this book.

never mind an album of family portraits. Indeed, photography was confined to luxury status within a predominantly agricultural society like Palestine. Added to this is the diaspora, the exile of 1948, the scattering far and wide of people and their belongings—including their photographs.

We had the luck of finding Professor Johnny Mansour from Haifa, a devoted chronicler of his city and its history, who like Ariadne in Greek mythology has committed himself to unspooling the photographic "thread of memory"* until it forms a collection of images. Mansour began revealing to us, bit by bit, photographs he'd gathered going from house to house, family to family, these small photographic jewels appearing in our inbox. Teresa and I decided we'd go to Haifa in search of the treasure.

Before meeting with Johnny in Haifa, we spent some time searching for other family albums and visiting friends in Ramallah, Bethlehem, and Jerusalem. This was on the eve of Operation Protective Edge in Gaza, when the Israeli army, backed by settlers, "combed" through the West Bank in search of three teenage Israeli settlers around the area of Hebron. In the summer of 2014, the West Bank was once again ransacked, turned upside down, with checkpoints closed, settlers blocking the roads, and raids taking place throughout the zone, while the bodies once again piled high on the Palestinian side. We'd sensed on arrival something was afoot from the unusual friendliness at Tel Aviv airport.

In Haifa, we enjoyed the warm welcome of many "48 Palestinians," the name used colloquially for Palestinian citizens of Israel, those not completely exiled—an active, unified community of resistance. There, we attended various political events, including a march in support of political prisoners; we were outraged to see for ourselves how the ancient city of Acre, a World Heritage Site, is intentionally falling into ruin, and we witnessed the constant bombardment and destruction of Haifa, the Arab city that came into existence long before 1948. On a hill there, overlooking the sea, we gazed down upon the family home of author and freedom fighter Ghassan Kanafani. It was abandoned, its inhabitants exiled. His descendants, like so many others, had become refugees.

The challenges presented by this research explain why most of the family photos come from the urban bourgeoisie of Haifa. While our intention with this book was never to conduct a sort of "photographic census" of Palestinian society, these albums presented by themselves would have provided only a partial, even distorted image. We had to place this collection of portraits in a broader framework of images that would bring us closer to the Palestine of those years in which the expulsion and ethnic cleansing of its inhabitants was brewing.

Following the trail of images, we'd find more treasure in the photographic archive of the American Colony Hotel in Jerusalem, known as the Matson Collection, an immense collection of more than 22,000 negatives and glass plates, many of

---

* Aranguren, *Palestina: el hilo de la memoria.*

them stereoscopic images, and most of them from Palestine. This collection is from the US Library of Congress, and most of the negatives and plates have been digitized and are freely accessible through their website.

The photographs that make up this collection were taken between 1898 and 1946 and include portraits of people in traditional dress, celebrities, events of social and political significance—including several uprisings against Zionist invasion—as well as images of local festivals, of factories, of workers. These images of such quality and beauty were for me as a photographer a dream to behold, a discovery that filled us with enthusiasm, allowing us to close the circle.

⁓A Few Technical Notes⁓

It is difficult, at times impossible, to note an exact date for the photos in this book. Some of the images belonging to the Matson Collection, for example, do record the date they were taken or the publication date, and we have also maintained data denoting a much broader time period. Each time we discovered a date scribbled in pencil on the back of a photo, it was a relief, a delight, to be able to create a temporal link to the political context shaping Palestine at the time.

In the images digitized directly from the negative or plate, we decided to maintain the film's black frame, with its numbering, and with what in some cases appear to be traces of adhesive tape, as we feel this contributes documentary value. Particularly notable are the annotations with dates and information from the places where they were taken. And while notes appear inverted in the photograph, they are exposed (pun intended) if viewed through a mirror. This is the case with those belonging to the Matson Collection, for which we also include various stereoscopic photographs in their entirety, while mostly using half of the entire image, as this method involves making a double image of the same subject.

To preserve the feel, the character, of family photo albums, we included the mounts used to frame the images, the same card that formed the pages of the albums, sometimes including their inscriptions. These pages of wrinkled, folded card paper and the images they hold reveal wear and tear—the reason we decided not to photoshop or clean up these folds, stains, or marks, traces of hands turning the pages and beholding memories—to respect the imprints of the various generations found within these portraits.

Sandra Barrilaro, Photographer

The 418 Palestinian Villages Destroyed in 1948–1949

Acre District
Iqrit
Umm al-Faraj
al-Birwa
al-Bassa
Tarbikha
al-Tall
Khirbat Jiddin
Khirbat 'Iribbin
al-Damun
Dayr al-Qasi
al-Ruways
al-Zib
Suhmata
Suruh
al-Sumayriyya
'Arab al-Samniyya
'Amqa
al-Ghabisiyya
al-Kabri
Kufr 'Inan
Kuwaykat
al-Manshiyya
al-Mansura
Miar
al-Nabi Rubin
al-Nahr

Bisan District
al-Ashrafiyya
Umm 'Ajra
al-Bira
Tall al-Shawk
Jabbul
al-Hamra
al-Hamidiyya
Khirbat Umm Sabuna
Khirbat al-Zawiya
Khirbat al-Taqa
al-Khunayzir
Danna
Zab'a
al-Sakhina
al-Samiriyya
Sirin
al-Tira
'Arab al-Bawati
'Arab al-Safa
'Arab al-'Arida
al-Ghazzawiyya
al-Fatur
Farwana
Qumya
Kafra
Kawkab al-Hawa
al-Murassas

Masil al-Jizl
Yubla

Beersheba District
al-Jammama
al-Khalasa
al-'Imara

Gaza District
Isdud
Barbara
Barqa
Burayr
al-Batani al-Sharqi
al-Batani al-Gharbi
Bi'lin
Bayt Jirja
Bayt Daras
Bayt Tima
Bayt 'Affa
Tall al-Turmus
Jusayr
al-Jaladiyya
al-Jura
Julis
al-Jiyya
Hatta
Hulayqat

Hamama
al-Khisas
Dimra
Dayr Sunayd
Simsim
al-Sawafir al-Sharqiyya
al-Sawafir al-Shamaliyya
al-Sawafir al-Gharbiyya
Summil
'Iraq Suwaydan
'Iraq al-Manshiyya
'Arab Suqrir
al-Faluja
Qastina
Karatiyya
Kawfakha
Kawkaba
al-Muharraqa
al-Masmiyya al-Saghira
al-Masmiyya al-Kabira
Najd
Ni'ilya
Hiribya
Huj
Yasur
'Ibdis

Haifa District
Abu Zurayq
Abu Shusha
Ijzim
Umm al-Zinat
Umm al-Shawf
Barrat Qisarya
Burayka
al-Butaymat
Balad al-Shaykh
Jaba'
al-Jalama
Khubbayza
Khirbat al-Burj
Khirbat al-Damun
Khirbat Sa'sa'
Khirbat al-Sarkas
Khirbat al-Shuna
Khirbat al-Kasayir
Khirbat Qumbaza
Khirbat Lid
Khirbat al-Manara
Khirbat al-Mansura
Daliyat al-Rawha'
al-Rihaniyya
al-Sindiyana
al-Sawamir
Sabbarin

al-Sarafand
al-Tantura
al-Tira
Arab Zahrat al-Dumayri
'Arab al-Fuqara'
'Arab al-Nufay'at
'Ayn Ghazal
'Ayn Hawd
al-Ghubayya al-Tahta
al-Ghubayya al-Fawqa
Qannir
Qira
Qisarya
Kabara
Kafr Lam
al-Kafrayn
al-Mazar
al-Mansi
al-Naghnaghiyya
Hawsha
Wadi 'Ara
Wa'arat al-Sarris
Yajur
Atlit

Hebron District

Khirbat Umm Burj
Barqusya
Bayt Jibrin
Bayt Nattif
Tall al-Safi
al-Dawayima

Dayr al-Dubban
Dayr Nakhkhas
Ra'na
Zakariyya
Zikrin
Zayta
'Ajjur
al-Qubayba
Kudna
Mughallis

Jaffa District

al-'Abbasiyya
Abu Kishk
Bayt Dajan
Biyar 'Adas
Fajja
al-Haram
Ijlil al-Qibliyya
Ijlil al-Shamaliyya
al-Jammasin al-Gharbi
al-Jammasin al-Sharqi
Jarisha
al-Khayriyya
Rantiya
al-Safiriyya
Saqiya
Salama
al-Sawalima
al-Sheikh Muwannis
Kafr 'Ana
al-Mirr

al-Mas'udiyya
al-Muwaylih
Yazur

Jerusalem District

Sataf
al-Qastal
Suba
Bayt 'Itab
Bayt Mahsir
Lifta
Khirbat al-Lawz
Dayr al-Shaykh
Dayr Yasin
Qalunya
al-Walaja
al-Maliha
'Ayn Karim
Dayr Rafat
Dayr al-Hawa
Saris
Bayt Naqquba
'Allar
'Aqqur
'Artuf
Bayt 'Itab
Bayt Thul
Bayt Umm al-Mays
al-Burayj
Dayr Aban
Dayr 'Amr
Ishwa'

Islin
Khirbat Ism Allah
Jarash
al-Jura
Kasla
Nitaf
al-Qabu
Ras Abu 'Ammar
Sar'a
Sufla
Khirbat al-Tannur
Khirbat al-'Umur

Jenin District

'Ayn al-Mansi
Khirbat al-Jawfa
al-Lajjun
al-Mazar
Nuris
Zir'in

Nazareth District

Saffuriyya
Indur
al-Mujaydil
Ma'lul

Ramleh District

Abu al-Fadl
Abu Shusha
'Ajanjul
'Aqir

Barfiliya
al-Barriyya
Bashshit
Khirbat Bayt Far
Bayt Jiz
Bayt Nabala
Bayt Shanna
Bayt Susin
Bir Ma'in
Bir Salim
al-Burj
Khirbat al-Buwayra
Daniyal
Dayr Abu Salama
Dayr Ayyub
Dayr Muhaysin
Dayr Tarif
Khirbat al-Duhayriyya
al-Haditha
Idnibba
Innaba
Jilya
Jimzu
Kharruba
al-Khayma
Khulda
al-Kunayyisa
al-Latrun
al-Maghar
Majdal Yaba
al-Mansura
al-Mukhayzin

al-Muzayri'a
al-Na'ani
al-Nabi Rubin
Qatra
Qazaza
al-Qubab
Qubayba
Qula
Sajad
Salbit
Sarafand al-'Amar
Sarafand al-Kharab
Saydun
Shahma
Shilta
al-Tina
al-Tira
Umm Kalkha
Wadi Hunayn
Yibna
Khirbat Zakariyya
Zarnuqa

Safad District
Abil al-Qamh
al-'Abisiyya
'Akbara
'Alma
'Ammuqa
'Arab al-Shamalina
'Arab al-Zubayd
'Ayn al-Zaytun

Baysamun
Biriyya
al-Butayha
al-Buwayziyya
Dallata
al-Dawwara
Dayshum
al-Zahiriyya al-Tahta
al-Dirbashiyya
al-Dirdara
Fara
al-Farradiyya
Fir'im
Ghabbatiyya
Ghuraba
al-Hamra'
Harrawi
Hunin
al-Husayniyya
Jahula
al-Ja'una
Jubb Yusuf
Kafr Bir'im
al-Khalisa
Khan al-Duwayr
Khirbat Karraza
al-Khisas
Khiyam al-Walid
Kirad al-Baqqara
Kirad al-Ghannama
Lazzaza
Madahil

al-Malikiyya
Mallaha
al-Manshiyya
al-Mansura
Mansurat al-Khayt
Marus
Mirun
al-Muftakhira
Mughr al-Khayt
Khirbat al-Muntar
al-Nabi Yusha'
al-Na'ima
Qabba'a
Qadas
Qaddita
Qaytiyya
al-Qudayriyya
al-Ras al-Ahmar
Sabalan
Safsaf
Saliha
al-Salihiyya
al-Sammu'i
al-Sanbariyya
Sa'sa
al-Shawka al-Tahta
al-Shuna
Taytaba
Tulayl
al-'Ulmaniyya
al-'Urayfiyya
al-Wayziyya

Yarda
al-Zanghariyya
al-Zawiya
al-Zuq al-Fawqani
al-Zuq al-Tahtani

Tiberias District
'Awlam
al-Dalhamiyya
Ghuwayr Abu Shusha
Hadatha
al-Hamma
Hittin
Kafr Sabt
Lubya
Ma'dhar
al-Majdal
al-Manara
al-Manshiyya
al-Mansura
Nasser al-Din
Nimrin
al-Nuqayb
Samakh
al-Samakiyya
al-Samra
al-Shajara
al-Tabigha
al-'Ubaydiyya
Wadi al-Hamam
Khirbat al-Wa'ra al-Sawda'
Yaquq

Tulkarm District
Khirbat Bayt Lid
Bayyarat Hannun
Fardisya
Ghabat Kafr Sur
al-Jalama
Kafr Saba
Khirbat al-Majdal
Khirbat al-Manshiyya
Miska
Qaqun
Raml Zayta
Tabsur
Umm Khalid
Wadi al-Hawarith
Wadi Qabbani
Khirbat al-Zababida
Khirbat Zalafa

Source: Walid Khalidi, ed., *All That Remains: The Palestinian Villages Occupied and Depopulated by Israel in 1948* (Washington, DC: Institute for Palestine Studies, 1992).

23

Photographs

صور

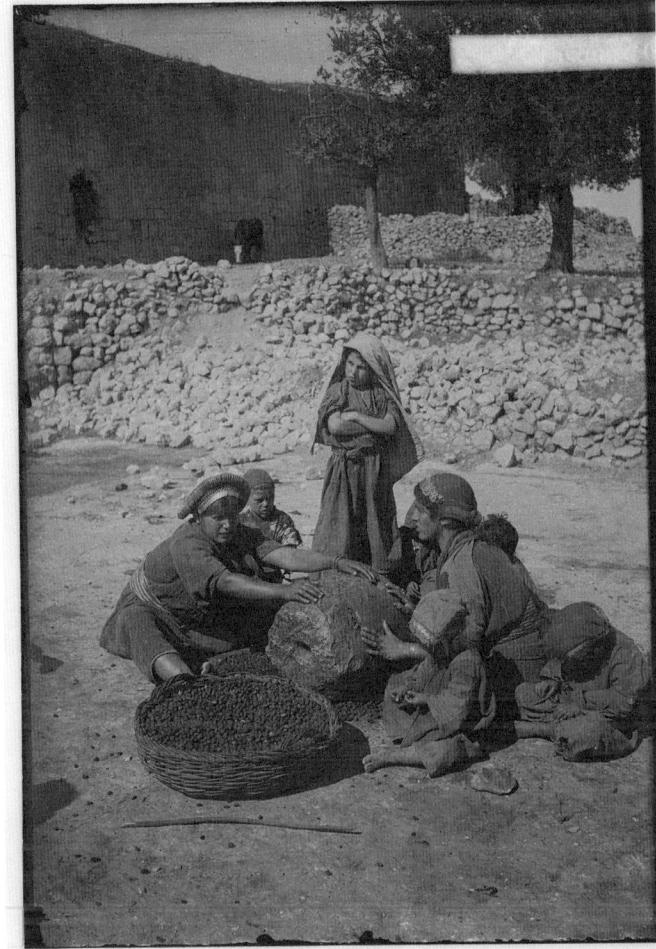

The traditional cultivation of olive trees in Palestine, 1934–1939.

Left: Olive tree pruning. Right: Women pressing olives, 1900–1920.

عدة صور حول زراعة الزيتون التقليدية في فلسطين، إلى اليسار عملية تقليم اشجار الزيتون، التقطت هذه الصور خلال الفترة من عام 1934 إلى 1939.

إلى اليمن نشاهد سيدات يقمن برص الزيتون. أخذت هذه الصورة خلال الفترة 1900 إلى 1920.

Left: Water wheel, 1900–1920.

Right: Women collecting olives from the ground, 1900–1920.

طاحونة شرقية تستخدم للري صورة تعود للفترة من 1900 و-1920.

نساء فلسطينيات يجمعن الزيتون من على الأرض،الصورة تعود إلى الفترة 1900 إلى 1920.

From abroad, we are accustomed to believe that Eretz Israel is presently almost totally desolate, an uncultivated desert, and that anyone wishing to buy land there can come and buy all he wants. But in truth, it is not so. In the entire land, it is hard to find tillable land that is not already tilled: only sandy fields and stony hills, suitable at best for planting trees or vine.*

لقد اعتدنا، نحن الذين نعيش خارج إسرائيل على الاعتقاد،بأنالأرض هناك صحراء قاحلة ولا تصلح للزراعة، وأن أي شخص يرغب في تملك أرض فهو متاح له بدون أية صعوبة. ولكن الواقع مغاير لذلك تماما. فنى طول البلاد وعرضها، من الصعب أن تجد أرضا صالحة للزراعة غير مزروعة. فليس هناك أرض غير مزروعة سوى الفيافي أو الجبال الصخرية التي لا تصلح للزراعة.

---

* Ehad Ha'am, pen name of Russian Jewish writer Asher Ginsberg, *Truth from Eretz Israel*, 1891.

There are extensive forests of pomegranate, orange, lemon, apple, sugarcane and palm trees. Its beautiful gardens have a great variety of plants, orchards with all kinds of legumes and vegetables, all nourished with water drawn by a multitude of waterwheels. Nature is prodigious ... It has some extraordinary gardens that provide possibly the first oranges in the world ... These are the best orange groves in the world.

هناك غابات واسعة من اشجار البرتقال اللّمون والتفاح وقصب السكر والنخيل. حدائقها تحتوي على أصناف مختلفة من النباتات ، مزارعها مليئة بمختلف أنواع البقوليات والخضروات،ثروى بمياه تستخرج بواسطة نواعير من آبار ارتوازية. الطبيعة جذابة .. . هناك بساتين تمتاز بجمال غير عادي ، وربما يكون هذا المكان هو مصدر أول ثمار البرتقال في العالم .. فيه افضل انواع البرتقال في العالم بدون شك. 2

* Fernández Sánchez and Freire Barreiro, *Santiago, Jerusalem, Rome*

American Colony / Jerusalem — 308 Jaffa from Hotel du Parc. Jaffa vom Hotel du Parc. Jaffa prise de l'Hotel du Parc.

Jaffa, one of the oldest cities in the world, was also one of the most populous cities in Palestine. One of its main activities was the cultivation of oranges. The cultivation of this fruit was a source of labor from harvest to export.

يافا واحدة أعرق المدن في العالم، وأكثر المدن الفلسطينية ازدحاما بالسكان. اشتهرت هذه المدينة بزارعة البرتقال. كان هذا المحصول يوفر فرص رئيسية للعمل ابتداء من قطف ثمار الحمضيات وحتى اعدادها للتصدير. ١

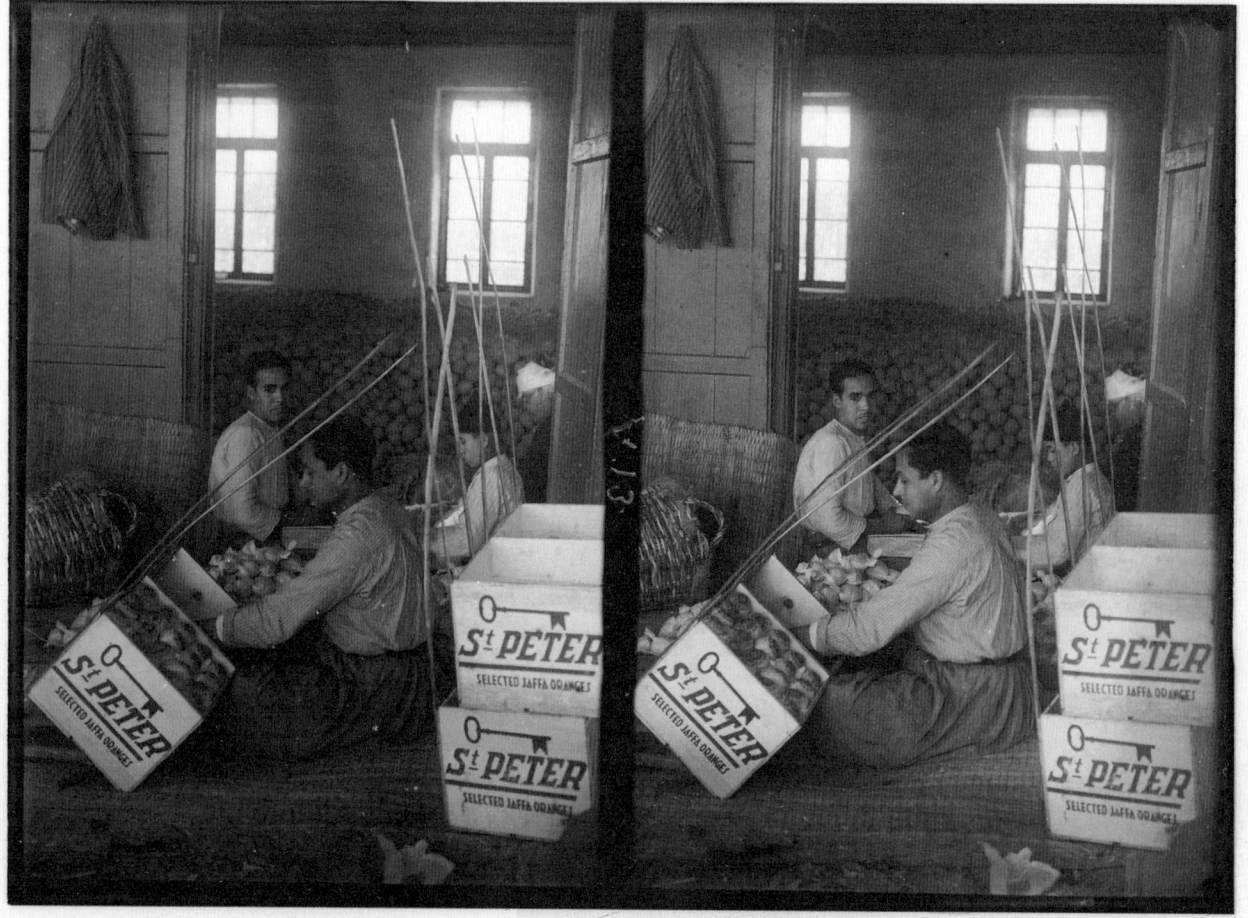

The culture of orange growing in Jaffa. Left: An orange grove with irrigation channels. Right: Men packing oranges into boxes, 1900–1920.

صور تُظهر ثقافة البرتقال في يافا. إلى اليسار بيارات البرتقال تشقها قنوات الري. وإلى اليمين رجال يقومون بتعبئة البرتقال في صناديق. هذه الصور تعود الى الفترة بين 1900و 1920.

Drying hides as part of the tanning process to prepare them for use as water containers, in Hebron, 1898–1914.

دباغة الجلود تحت اشعة الشمس للاستخدام :كأواني للماء في الخليل خلال الفترة بين 1989–1898, 1914.

*Hebron. It has large vineyards. It is in a fertile and lush valley whose grapes are especially famous. It is a town devoted to agriculture and the elaboration of objects of worship. There are olive groves and vineyards, planted with barley in a peaceful valley. Its inhabitants carefully cultivate their area and obtain large harvests of wine, barley and oil, golden wine.**

الخليل . تنتشر ببساتين العنب الواسعة. تقع في وادي خصب مليء بأشجار العنب التي تحظى بشهرة كبيرة .سكان المنطقة تخصصوا بالزراعة والصناعات اليدوية ذات المطابع الديني .تنتشر فيها اشجار الزيتون والعنب ، ومحصول. الشعير تتواجد بكثرة في هذا الوادي الوديع .سكان المنطقة يعتنون كثيرا بمزارعهم، التي تنتج محاصيل وفيرة من النبيذ والشعير والزيت.النبيذ الذهبي. 3

---

* Fernández Sánchez and Freire Barreiro, *Santiago, Jerusalem, Rome*

A melon market, 1900–1920.

سوق لبيع الشمام . تعود هذه الصورة الى الفترة من 1900 إلى 1920.

Agricultural production in 1946

(in dunums; one dunum equals 1,000 square meters)

Total area cultivated by Palestinians (with the exception of citrus fruits): 5,484,700 dunums.

Area cultivated by colonies of the Zionist movement: 425,450 dunums.

Cereals: Total area: 4,367,629 dunums. Palestinian property 4,152,438 dunums.

Bananas: 60 percent Palestinian owned.

Vineyards: 86 percent Palestinian owned.

Watermelons: Total area under cultivation 125,979 dunums, of which 120,304 dunums were Palestinian property.

Olive trees: Total area 600,133 dunums, 99 percent Palestinian owned.

Vegetables: Total crop area 279,940 dunums, of which 239,733 dunums were Palestinian owned.

Oranges: Palestinian property: 122,958 dunums; Zionist colonies: 114,352.[*]

الانتاج الزراعي [*]

مساحة الأرضي التي كان يفلحها الفلسطينيون (بدون الأخذ في الاعتبار تلك المزروعة بالحمضيات) ، بلغ 5.484.700 دونم (الدونم يعادل الف متر مربع).

مساحة الأرضي التابعة لمستعمرات الحركة الصهيونية 425.459 دونم.

مساحة الأرضي الفلسطينية المزروعة بالحبوب4.367.629 دونم . منها 4.152.438 دونم ملكية مزارعين فلسطينيين.

60% من الأراضي المزروعة بالموز ملكية فلسطينية. :

86% من الأراضي المزروعة بكروم العنب ، ملكية فلسطينية. :

إجمالي مساحة الأراضي مزروعة بالبطيخ تصل الى 125.979 دونم ، منها 120.304 ملكية فلسطينية.

مساحة الأراضي المزروعة بأشجار الزيتون:600.133 دونم، 99% ملكية فلسطينية.

مساحة الأرض المزروعة بالخضروات 279.940 دونم . منها 239.733 دونم من ملكية الفلسطينيين.

مساحة الأرضي المزروعة بالحمضيات:من ملكية فلسطينية بلغت :122.958 دونم . أما المستعمرات الصهيونية : 114.352.

* Anglo-American Committee of Inquiry, *A Survey of Palestine, 1946, Volume I*, cited in Walid Khalidi, *Before Their Diaspora: A Photographic History of the Palestinians, 1876–1948* (Beirut: Institute for Palestine Studies, 2010).

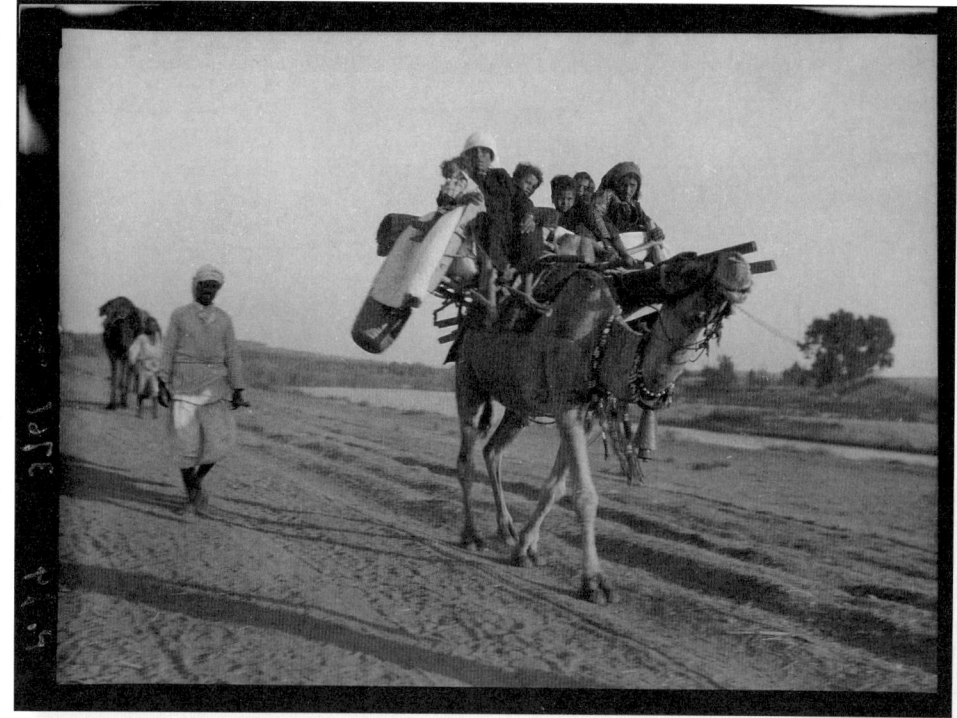

Left: Egyptian camel caravan crossing the Mount of Olives in 1918.

Right: Feast of the prophet Reuben in southern Palestine. Pilgrims on their way to visit the prophet's grave riding on camels, six women and children, camping equipment, 1920–1933.

قافلة مصرية من الجمال تجتاز جبل الزيتون 1918.

عيد النبي روبين بفلسطين جنوب. حجاج في طريقهم إلى زيارة قبر النبي ، على ظهر جمل. ستة نساء وأطفال بكل ما يلزم لنصب الخيمة. هذه الصورة تعود إلى الفترة بين 1920 و 1933.

The enchanting Lake Tiberias. The horses almost disappear under the bushes of purple hollyhocks and wild wheat and barley. There are many palm trees… It is the jewel of the Galilee.*

بحيرة طبرية الخلابة. الأحصنة تكاد تختفي خلف الشجيرات البنفسجية، والقمح والشعير البري. هناك عدد كبير من أشجار النخيل ... طبرية جوهرة الجليل.

* Fernández Sánchez and Freire Barreiro, *Santiago, Jerusalem, Rome.*

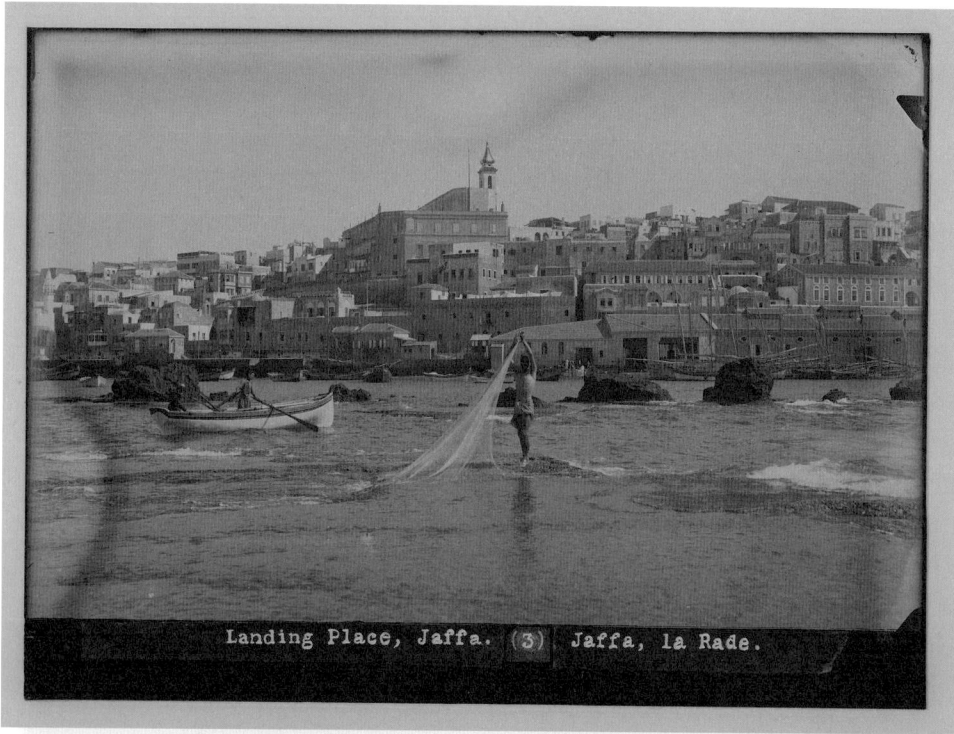

Landing Place, Jaffa. (3) Jaffa, la Rade.

Left: Trawling for fish in Jaffa, 1898–1914.

Right: Building the Jaffa pier, September 13, 1934.

يصيدون الأسماك في يافا خلال الفترة من 1898 و 1914.

يبنون رصيف ميناء يافا . التقطت هذه الصورة في 13 سبتمبر سنة 1934.

Left: A shopkeeper photographed in the entry to his shop in Jerusalem. Photograph dated between 1900 and 1920.

Right: Lemonade seller during the feast of the prophet Reuben in southern Palestine, 1920–1933.

صورة لتاجر في باب متجره في القدس. تعود الى الفترة 1900 إلى 1920.

بائع عصير الليمون خلال عيد النبي روبين في جنوب فلسطين . 1920 و 1933.

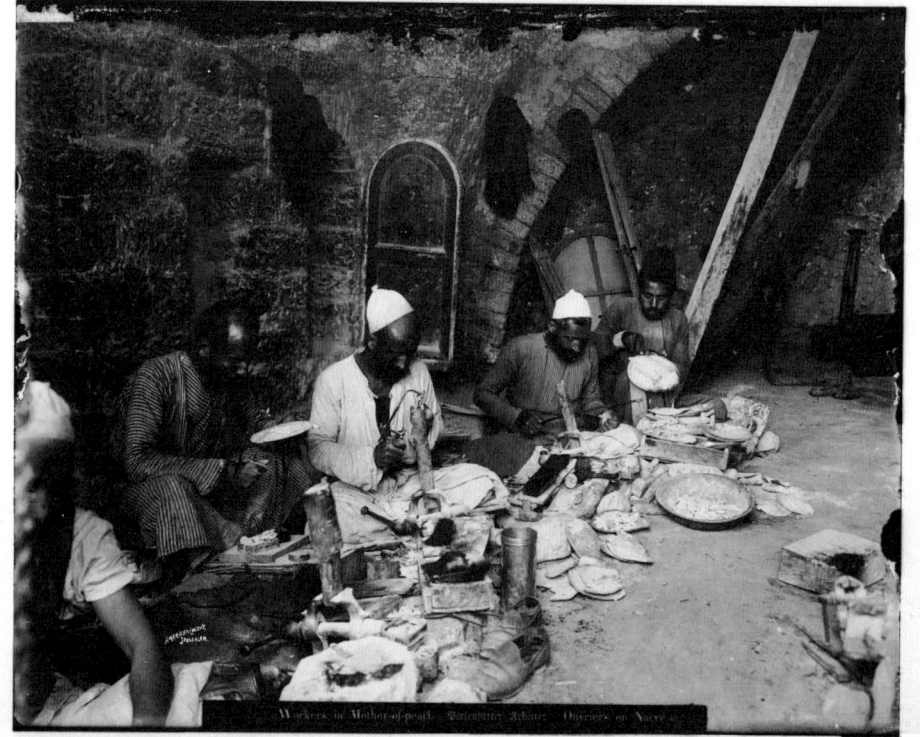

Left: A sculptor chopping olive wood for his carvings, 1934–1939.

Right: Several craftsmen working with mother-of-pearl in their workshop, 1898–1914.

نحات خشب يقوم بنشر خشب الزيتون من اجل تجسيمه . تعود الصورة إلى الفترة 1934 الى 1939.

عدد من الحرفين يعملون في تجسيم الناكار . خلال الفترة 1898 الى 1914.

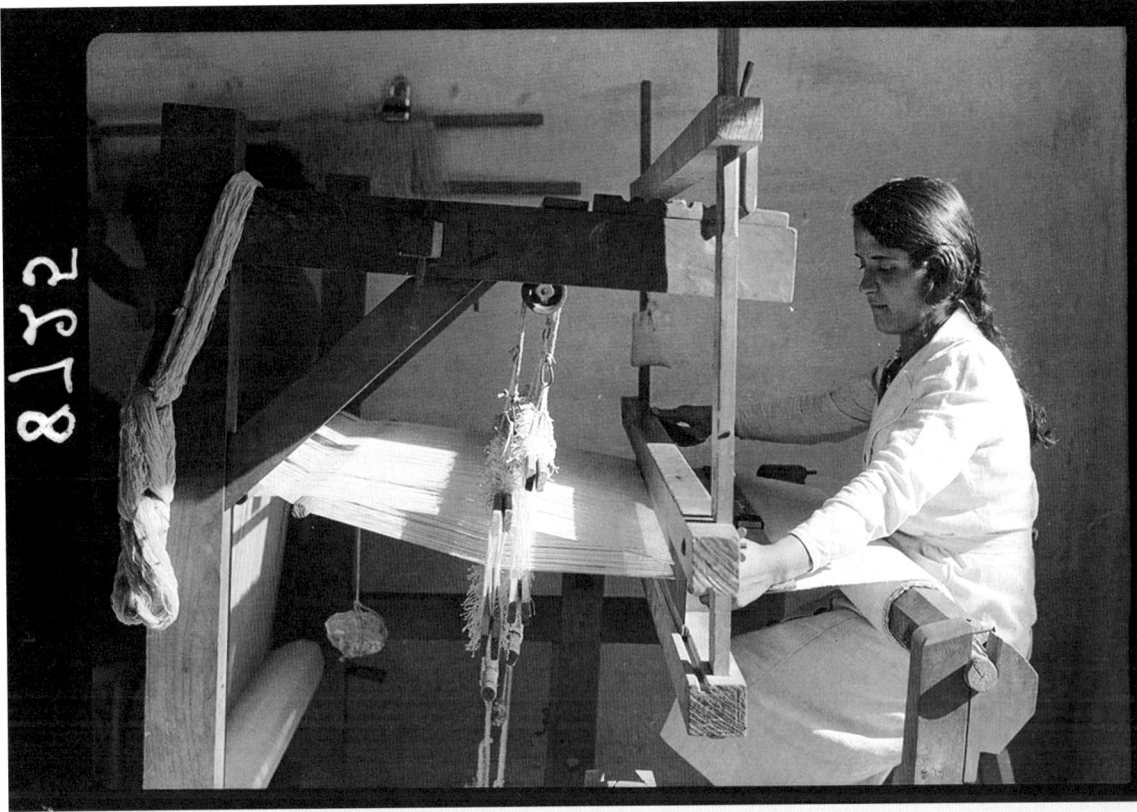

Young men and women working in the Women's Union workshop in Ramallah, 1934–1939.

صور تظهر شباب ونساء يعملون في معامل نسيج تابعة لاتحاد المرأة في رام الله . يعود تاريخها إلى الفترة بين 1934 و 1939.

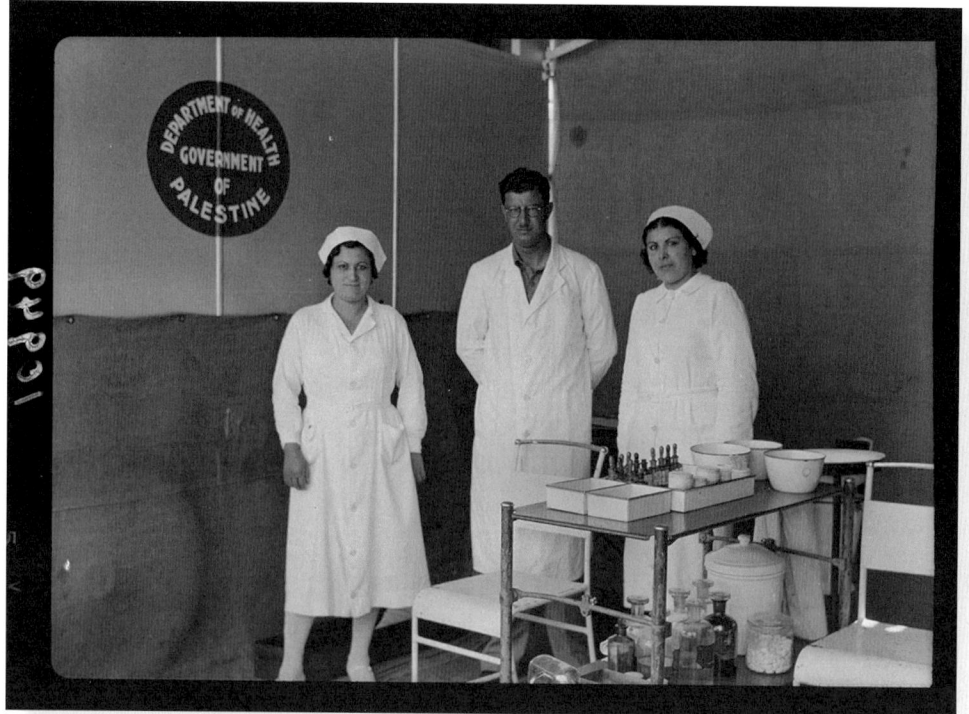

A mobile eye clinic from the Palestinian Government Department of Health, northeast of Gaza. August 1939.

الصورة التالية تبين صورا لعيادة متنقلة لطب العيون التابعة لقسم الصحة العامة بحكومة فلسطين ، اخذت خلال العمل في شمال شرق غزة بشهر اغسطس سنة 1939.

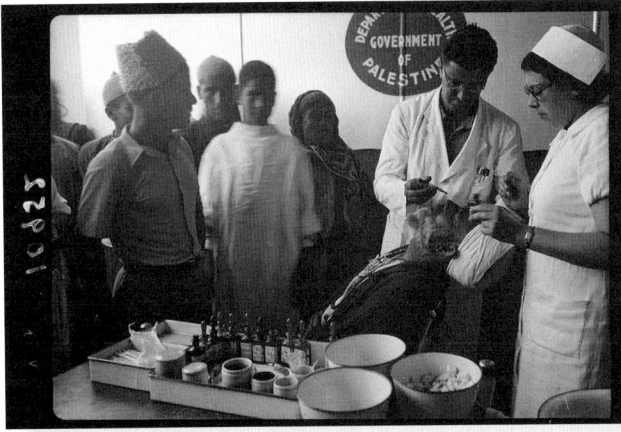

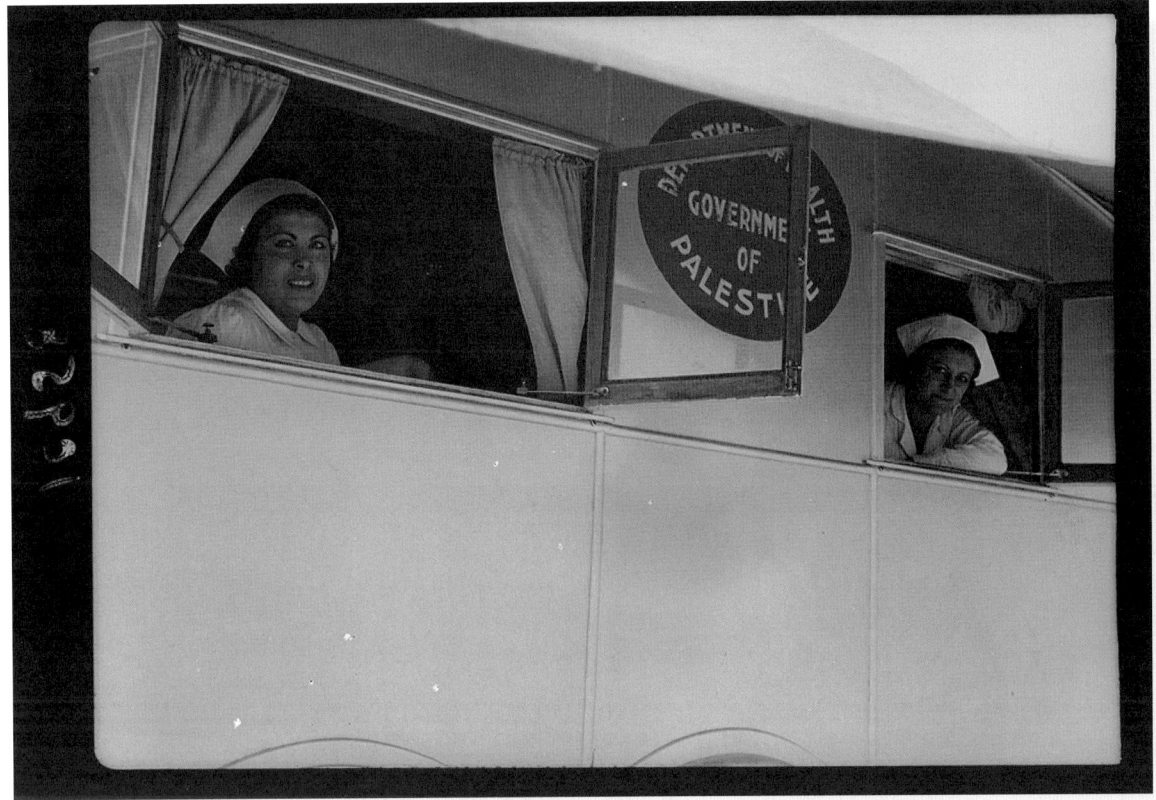

Top left: Doctor and nurse treating a patient. Bottom left: Dr. Shukeir with nurses and local Arabs. Right: Nurses leaning out of the caravan windows.

الدكتور شقير في صورة اخذت له برفقة الممرضات وعرب في المنطقة. ممرضات يطلن على من شبابيك الكرفان ، وصورة اخرى تظهر الكرفان بكامله. طبيب وممرضات يعاينون المرضى في المنطقة.

Hebron School for the Blind. 1940–1946.

صورة لمجموعة في مدرسة للمكفوفين في الخليل . تعود إلى الفترة 1940 – 1946.

Staff from Hebron hospital, run by Dr. Walker (nationality unknown). March 4, 1944.

طاقم مستشفى الخليل ، يترأسه الدكتور والكر (هويته غير محدده) . بتاريخ 4 مارس 1944.

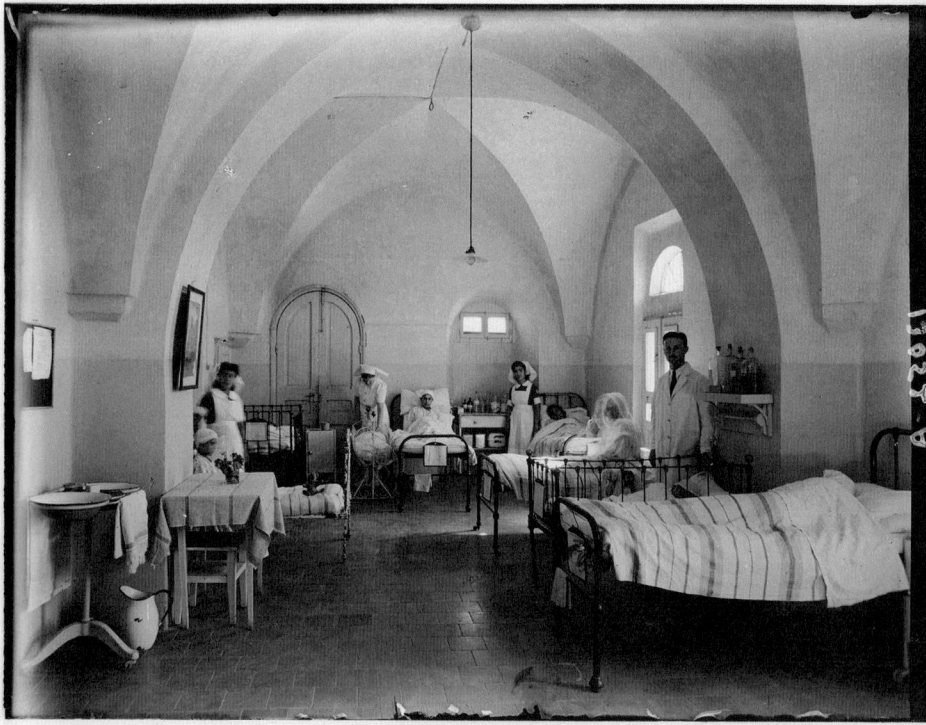

Hebron hospital. Left: The women's ward. Right: The nurses' dormitory. August 17, 1944.

صورتان لمستشفى الخليل اخذت في 17 اغسطس 1944. الصورة الأولى تبين جناح النساء والصورة الثانية يظهر فيها حجرة نوم الممرضات,.

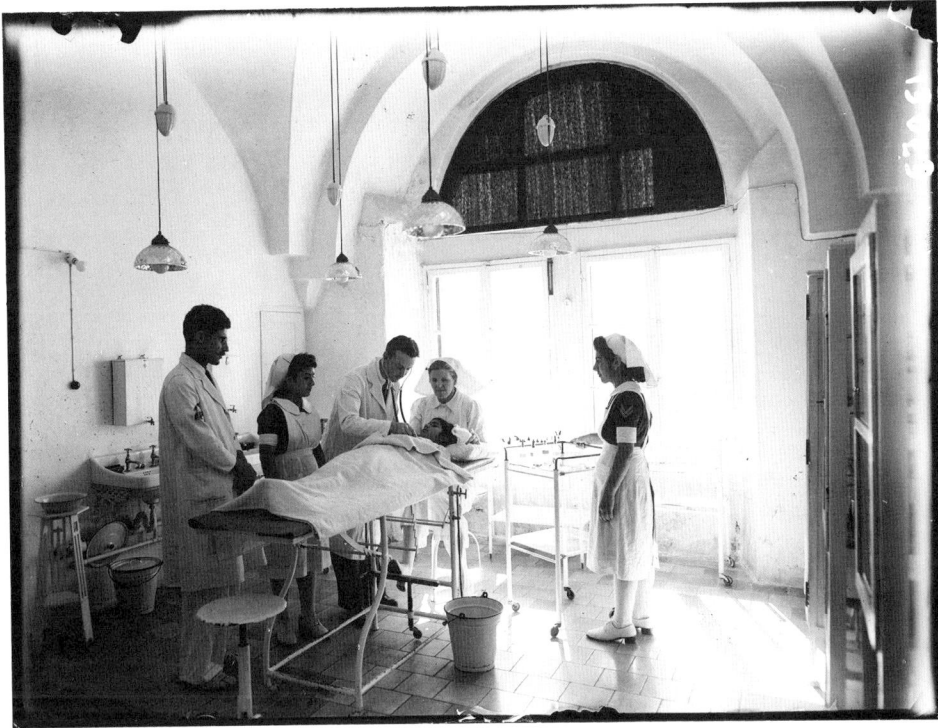

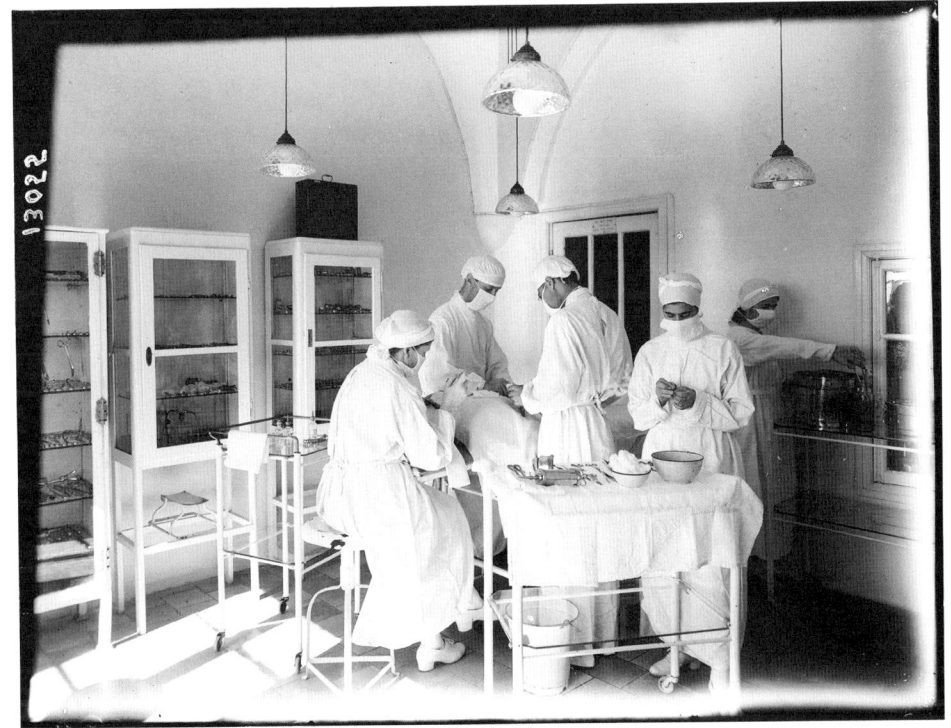

The operating room of the Hebron hospital. August 17, 1944.

صورتان لغرفة العمليات في مستشفى الخليل تعود الى تاريخ 17 اغسطس 1944.

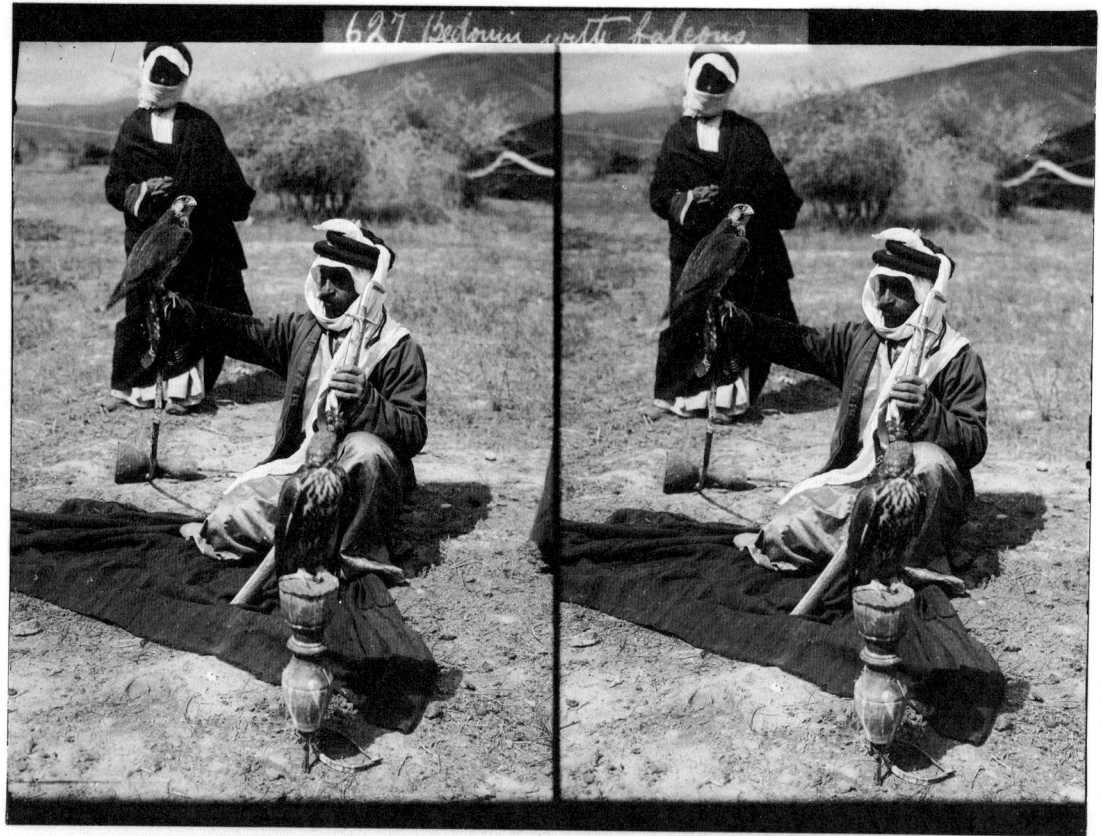

Left: Portrait of a Bedouin man, 1900–1910.

Right: Bedouins with a hunting falcon, 1900–1920.

صورة شخصية لبدوي أخذت خلال الفترة 1900- 1910 تقريبا.

بدو يحملون صقور للصيد اخذت الصورة خلال الفترة 1900 إلى 1920 تقريبا.

Left: The Armenian Patriarch in Jerusalem, 1900–1910.

Right: Armenian Church leader, 1900–1920.

بطرك الأرمن في القدس . أخذت بتاريخ 1900 – 1910.

زعيم الكنسية الأرمينية أخذت خلال الفترة 1900 إلى 1920.

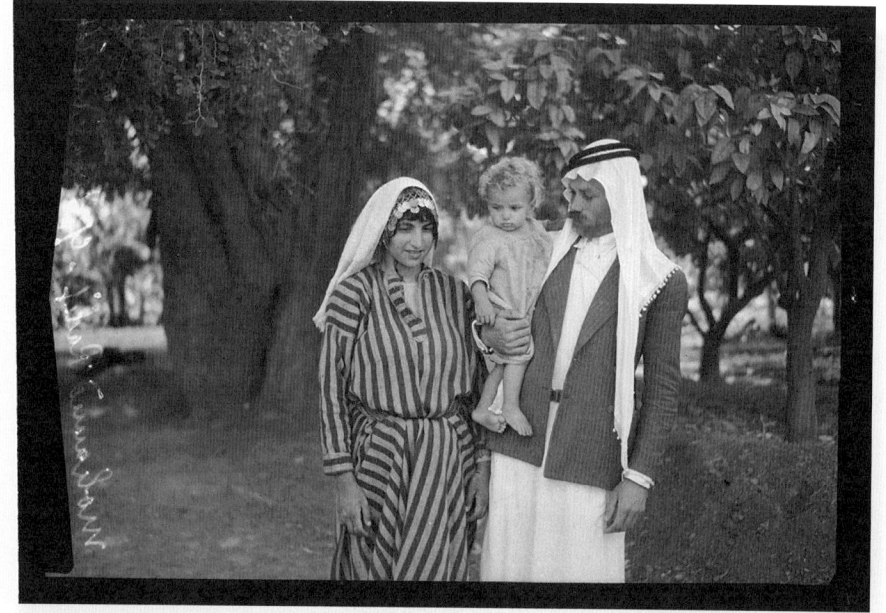

Left: Three generations from the village of Dhahiriyya (located between Hebron and Beersheba), February 9, 1940.

Right: Mahmud Radif and his family, April 28, 1946. Mr. Radif worked in Jericho for Ibrahim al-Naqib as a gardener.

ثلاثة اجيال من قرية الظهيرية ، الواقعة على الطريقة بين الخليل وبئر السبع اخذت بتاريخ 9 فبراير 1940.

صورة لمحمود رديف وعائلته . السيد رديف كان يعمل جنائني في أريحا عند إبراهيم النقيب. أخذت هذه الصورة في 28 ابريل 1946.

50

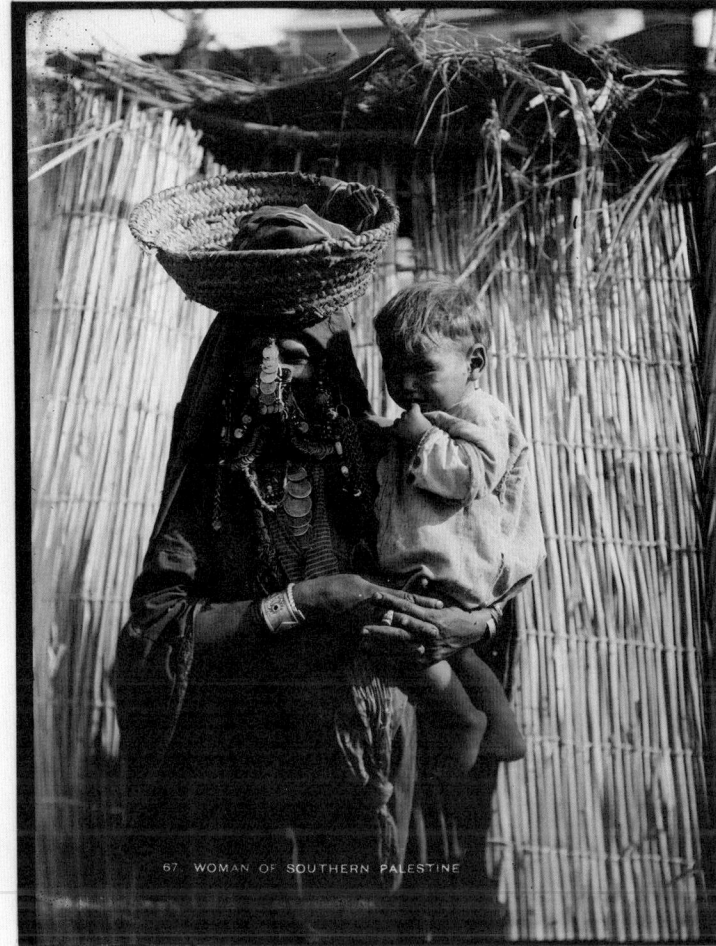

67. WOMAN OF SOUTHERN PALESTINE

Left: A Bedouin couple next to their tent, 1898–1914.

Right: A woman from the Beersheba area carrying a baby, 1900–1920.

صورة لزوج من البدو الى جانب خيمتهم . اخذت هذه الصورة خلال الفترة 1898 إلى 1914.

سيدة تحمل طفلها الرضيع بمنطقة بئر السبع اخذت او نشرت خلال الفترة 1900 إلى 1920.

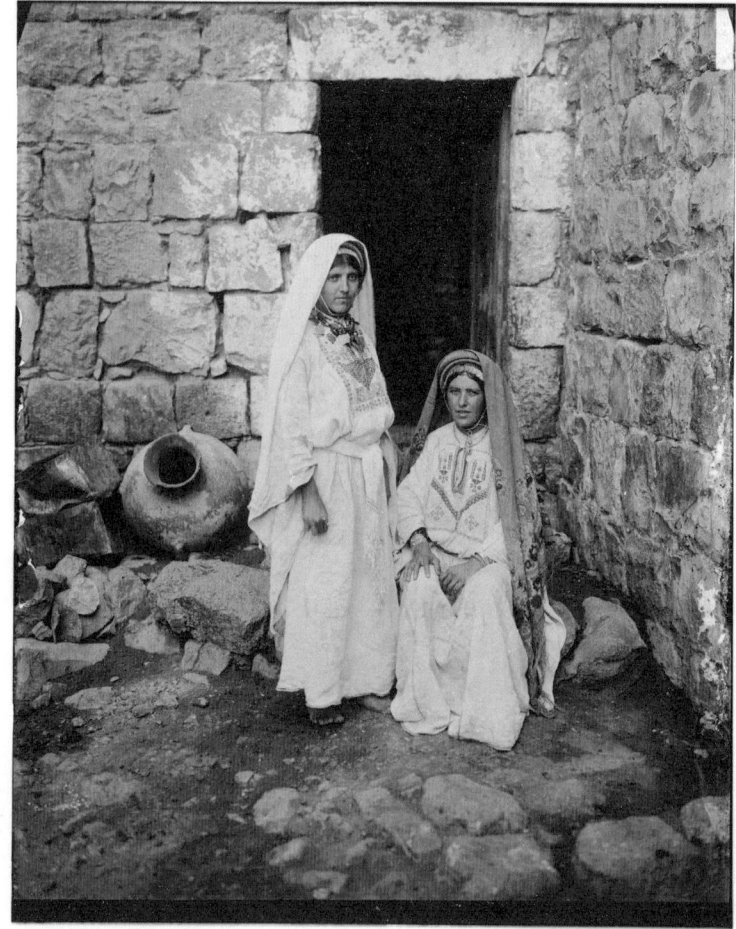

Arab women in traditional dress, 1900–1920. Left: Profile of a Ramallah woman.

Right: Two young women from the same town standing in front of the doorway of a house.

صورتان لسيدتين عربتين ترتديان اللباس التقليدي ، صورة جانبية لسيدة من رام الله . الصورة إلى اليمن تظهر شابتان من نفس المدينة تقفان أمام أحد البيوت . الصورتان تعودان الى فترة 1900 أو 1920.

A Ramallah woman dressed traditionally and carrying a pitcher, 1898–1920.

صورة لسيدة من رام الله ترتدي الزي التقليدي وتحمل جرة ماء . يعود تاريخ هذه الصورة الى الفترة 1898 الى 1920.

Left: A bride from Bethlehem, seated and accompanied by women and girls, 1900–1920.

Right: A woman and young girl seated near dolls in traditional Arab dress; one of the dolls bears a label with the inscription Ramallah Doll, 1920–1946.

صورة عروس من بيت لحم جالسة برفقة نساء وأطفال. الصورة تعود للفترة 1900 إلى 1920.

الصورة على اليمين تظهر سيدة وطفلة جالستان إلى جانب لعب بملابس عربية تقليدية. إحدى اللعب تحمل تيكت كتبت عليه:لعبة من رام الله , الصورة تعود الى الفترة 1920 الى 1946.

Three Bethlehem women sitting, smoking hookah, and drinking coffee in a private residence, 1898–1914.

الصورة تظهر ثلاث نساء من بيت لحم يدخن الأرجيله ، ويشربن القهوة في أحد البيوت. الصورة تعود للفترة 1898 الى 1914.

602 A Family of Bethlehem. Bethlehemiter Familie. Une Famille de Bethléem.

A Bethlehem family, 1898–1914.

صورة جميلة لعائلة من رام الله تاريخها 1898 الى 1914.

618 Peasant Family of Ramallah. Bauern-familie von Ramallah.

A Ramallah family, 1898–1914.

صورة جميلة لعائلة من رام الله تاريخها 1989 الى 1914.

580 Franciscan Monks. Franciscaner. Pères Latins

Left: A group of Franciscan monks, 1898–1914.

Right: A group of Coptic monks, 1898–1914.

الصورة الى اليسار لمجموعة رهبان من طائفة الفرنثيسكان.الصورة اليمني تظهر مجموعة من الرهبان الاقباط. تاريخ كلا
الصورتين الفترة 1898 الى 1914.

581 Greek Monks. Griechische Mönche. Des moines Grecs.

Left: Greek monks, 1898–1914.

Right: Druze women, 1898–1914.

رهبان يونانيون في الصورة على اليسار.

وفي يمينهن صورة لمجموعة من النساء الدُرزيات. تاريخ كلا الصورتين يعود الى الفترة 1898 الى 1914.

Left: The family of Subhi Taher Dajani, 1940–1946. He was the director of the Hebron School for the Blind.

Right: Acre State Stallion Farm staff in the garden of Jamil Pasha's house in Haifa, April 23, 1940.

فى الجانب الايسر نشاهد صورة لعائلة الدجانى صبحى طاهر الدجانى .الذى كان يعمل مديرا لمدرسة المكفوفين فى الخليل . تاريخ هذه الصورة 1940 الى 1946.

كادر يعمل فى المزرعة العامة والتى تربى فيها ذكور الحيوانات المحسنة والمعدة للتلقيح فى مدينة عكا. الصورة فى حديقة بيت جميل باشا فى حيفا . اخذت بتاريخ 23 أبريل 1940.

The Dajani family, 1940–1946.

صورة أخرى لعائلة الدجاني مؤرخة في الفترة 1940 إلى 1946.

An engineer transmits the broadcast marking the inauguration of the Palestine Broadcasting Service, March 30, 1936.

This first broadcast was attended by figures from the Mandate government, as well as Arthur Wauchope, High Commissioner of Palestine and the highest representative of British power in the area, who delivered a speech during the inaugural ceremony.

Wauchope indicated that the station would not cover political issues, but would focus on "knowledge and culture," a first indication of the future and limitations of radio broadcasting in Mandatory Palestine.*

افتتاح خدمات البث الإذاعي في فلسطين بتاريخ 30 مارس 1936.

ويظهر في الصورة أحد المهندسين المشرفين على متابعة البث.

حضر افتتاح أول بث إذاعي عدد من الشخصيات ومسئولين في حكومة الانتداب بمن فيهم المندوب السامي ارثور واوشوب الحاكم العام للانتداب في فلسطين، أعلى ممثل رسمي للحكومة البريطانية في المنطقة، حيث القى كلمة في حفل الافتتاح.

وقد ذَكَّر في كلمته بأن البث لن يتطرق إلى القضايا السياسية بل سيتركز على مواضيع "الثقافة والمعرفة" .بهذه الكلمات وما ورد عنه فيما بعد اوضح واوشوب الحدود التي يجب ان يقف عندها البث الاذاعي في فلسطين خلال الانتداب.

* Andrea Stanton, "Jerusalem Calling: The Birth of the Palestine Broadcasting Service," *Jerusalem Quarterly*, no. 50, Summer 2012. Also by the same author, *This Is Jerusalem Calling: State Radio in Mandate Palestine* (Austin: University of Texas Press, 2013).

The Palestine Broadcasting Service studios in Jerusalem, 1936–1946.

Left: Band performance. Right: A singer.

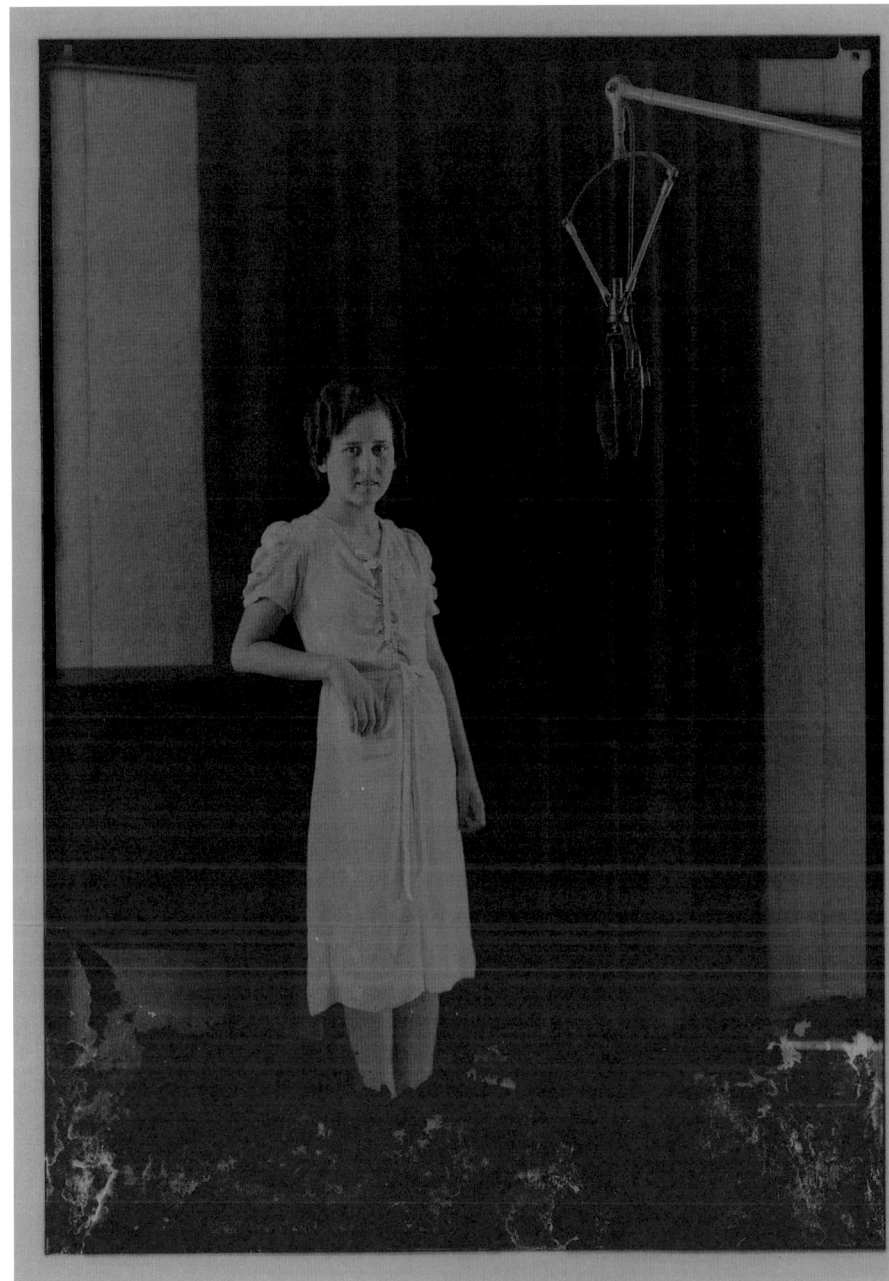

صورتان لفنانين فى استوديوهات البث الإذاعي الفلسطيني، فى القدس. صورة شخصية لمغنية ولفرقة غنائية خلال
اقامة حفلتيا. التاريخ:1936 إلى ، 1946.

Images from the Jerusalem studios of the Palestine Broadcasting Service. Left: A musician playing the 'oud. 1936–1946.

Right: A group of Arab musicians together with two soloists, a young girl and boy, at the microphone, 1940–1946.

لى اليسار موسيقار يعزف على العود مؤرخة في الفترة 1936 إلى 1946.

في الصورة على اليمين مجموعة من الموسيقيين العرب ، بجانب عازفين : طفل وطفلة امام الميكروفون . بتاريخ 1940 الى 1946.

64

More photographs from the Palestine Broadcasting Service. Left: Arab personnel with the musicians of a traditional Arab orchestra (Takht) during the farewell party for Mr. Tweedy (a British public information official), September 25 or 26, 1941.

Right: Some of the Arab employees of the Palestine Broadcasting Service, May 15, 1941.

مزيد من الصور من خدمات البث الإذاعي الفلسطيني. إلى اليسار جزء من العاملين العرب في صورة تجمعهم مع موسيقيين من جوقة موسيقية عربية تقليدية (تخت) خلال حفل توديع السيد تويدي (موظف بريطاني في قسم الخدمات الاخبار العامة). بتاريخ 25 أو 26 سبتمبر 1941.

صورة ثانية اخذت في مايو 41 وتظهر مجموعة كبيرة من الموظفين العرب.

The brand new Palestine Broadcasting Service studios in Queen Melisande's Way, Jerusalem.
Left: A group of engineers photographed on the entrance stairs, 1934–1939.

Right: A group of Arab employees from the Palestine Broadcasting Service, May 15, 1941.

استوديوهات جديدة لخدمات البث الإذاعي الفلسطيني في كوين ميلياندس واي في القدس . عدد من المهندسين أخذت لهم الصورة عند درج المدخل . مؤرخة خلال الفترة 1934 إلى 1939.

مجموعة من العرب العاملين في قسم خدمات البث الإذاعي الفلسطيني. اخذت لهم الصورة في 15 مايو 1941.

Left: Outside the Palestine Broadcasting Service studio with Ajaj Nuwayhed (head of the Arab section, second row, second from right) and Syrian nay player Samy Shawa (second row, third from right), 1934–1939.

Right: The Palestine Broadcasting Service team. Sheikh Mustafa al-Jilani (in the center) with Samy Bay al-Kilani and Shafik Bek Jabri. Ajaj Nuwayhed is standing.

مجموعة صُورت خارج استوديوهات اذاعة فلسطين برفقة عجاج اف (رئيس القسم العربية وفي الصف الثاني رقم 2 من اليمين)، عازف الناي السوري سامي شوا (الصف الثاني ، الثالث من اليمين) 1934-1939.

صورة لمجموعة من العاملين في الاذاعة الفلسطينية ، اخذت في 8 اغسطس سنة 1942. عرب. الشيخ مصطفى الجيلاني (في الوسط) الى جانب سامي بيك الكيلاني ، شفيق بيك جبري ، واقفا عجاج اف .

Left: Reception of the Director of Programs of the Palestine Broadcasting Service in which the traditional Arab orchestra (Takht) performed as guests were being received, May 6, 1940.

Right: A Palestine Broadcasting Service party in Jericho with a performance of the Arab Legion band; Jordan Hotel is in the background, May 6, 1940.

حفلة في أريحا اقامها البث الإذاعي الفلسطيني . حيث عزفت فرقة الجيش العربي، يلاحظ من بعيد فندق الأردن . بتاريخ 6 مايو 1940.

استقبال مدير البرامج في خدمات البث الإذاعي الفلسطيني.حيث عزفت جوقة الموسيقي العربية التقليدية (تخت) خلال استقبال المدعوين . بتاريخ 6 مايو 1940.

Left: An open-air cinema in the village of Halhul, 30 kilometers from Hebron. A large crowd attends the projection on an outer wall of the mosque, July 1, 1940.

Right: The open-air film projection in Halhul, with a group of women in the background.

صالة عرض سينمائية في الهواء الطلق في قرية حلحول التي تبعد 30 كلم عن الخليل. عدد كبير من الحاضرين لمساعدة عرض الفيلم على حائط المسجد الخارجي . بتاريخ 1 يوليو 1940.

صورة أخرى من العرض السينمائي في الهواء الطلق ببلدة حلحول . يشاهد عن بعد عدد كبير من النساء.

Left: Solidarity meeting in Hebron. Authorities are photographed on the roof of a school and include Keith Roach, director of the Department of Antiquities of the Palestinian Government during the British Mandate (center), and the Mufti of Hebron, July 3, 1940.

Right: A crowd in Tiberias waits for the first seaplane to land on the Sea of Galilee, October 1931.

لقاء تضامني في الخليل، مجموعة من المسئولين يتصورن على سطح المدرسة . السيد كيث رواش مدير قسم الآثار في الحكومة الفلسطينية خلال الانتداب البريطاني مع مفتي الخليل . هذه الصورة مأخوذة 3 يوليو 1940.

طائرات من شركة الخطوط الجوية إمبريال المحدودة في بحر الجليل في سماخ. الجماهير تنتظر في طبرية ان تحط أول طائرة للتزود بالماء في بحر الجليل . اكتوبر 1931.

Left: A foundation stone-laying ceremony for the Ramallah municipal school on November 23, 1940. Keith Roach, director of the Department of Antiquities of the Palestinian Government during the British Mandate, is seated in the center.

Right: Keith Roach's car passes two rows of Palestinian Boy Scouts as he leaves after the foundation stone-laying ceremony for the Ramallah municipal school.

حفل خلال وضع الحجر الأول في مشروع بناء مدرسة بلدية رام الله بتاريخ 23 نوفمبر 1940. يشاهد جالسا في وسط الجمع السيد كيث رواتش مدير قسم الآثار بالحكومة الفلسطينية خلال الانتداب البريطاني.

سيارة السيد كيث رواتش تجتاز صفين من صفوف الكشافة بعد مغادرة المكان بانتهاء الحفل الخاص بوضع حجر الاساس في مشروع مدرسة بلدية رام الله.

Left: Muslim celebrations in Wady Nemil in al-Majdal. Seyid Hussein Shireen is in the al-Muntar neighborhood of Gaza. Procession in Seyid Hussein. Festivities celebrated April 20 and 22, 1943.

Right: Photograph of the same procession from al-Majdal to Seyid Hussein, April 21, 1943.

حفل إسلامي في المجدل، وادي النمل، السيد حسين شرين في حي المنطار بغزة. استعراض السيد الحسين. تم الاحتفال بهذه الأعياد خلال الفترة 20 إلى 22 أبريل سنة 1943.

صورة من الاستعراض بين المجدل والسيد الحسين أقيم بتاريخ 21 أبريل سنة 1943.

Left: The Quaker mission school in Ramallah, May 25, 1937.

Right: A member of the Nuseiba family opens the door to the Church of the Holy Sepulchre in Jerusalem, 1900–1902. For centuries, the various Christian sects competed for custody of the key to the Holy Sepulchre. Being in charge of the daily opening and closing of the doors of the most important church in Christendom had led even to physical fights between Catholic, Orthodox, Armenian, Coptic, and other Christians. In the nineteenth century, notable Christians of Jerusalem adopted a Solomonic decision: the key to the Church of the Holy Sepulchre would be placed in the hands of a prominent Muslim family from Jerusalem, the Nuseibas, who would be in charge of opening and closing the door of the Holy Sepulchre each day. This practice continues to this day.

التقطت هذه الصورة بتاريخ 25 مايو 1937 في مدرسة بعثة "كواكيرا" في رام الله.

تنافست مختلف الطوائف المسيحية طول قرون على حيازة مفتاح كنيسة القيامة. إذا أن التحكم في فتح وإغلاق أبواب أهم كنسية من كنائس العالم المسيحي يوميا، كان سببا في خلافات وصلت الى حد الصراع الجسدي بين الكاثوليك، والارثودوكس، والأرمن، والأقباط ..الخ . وقد انتهى الصراع في القرن التاسع عشر عندما اهتدى زعماء هذه الطوائف المسيحية إلى حل وسط يمثل في تكليف أحدى العائلات المسلمة المعتبرة في القدس (عائلة النسيبة) بمهمة الإشراف على المفاتيح وتتولى فتح وإغلاق ابواب كنيسة القيامة يوميا.
نظهر الصورة أحد ابناء عائلة نسيبة خلال فتح أبواب كنيسة القيامة سنة 1920.

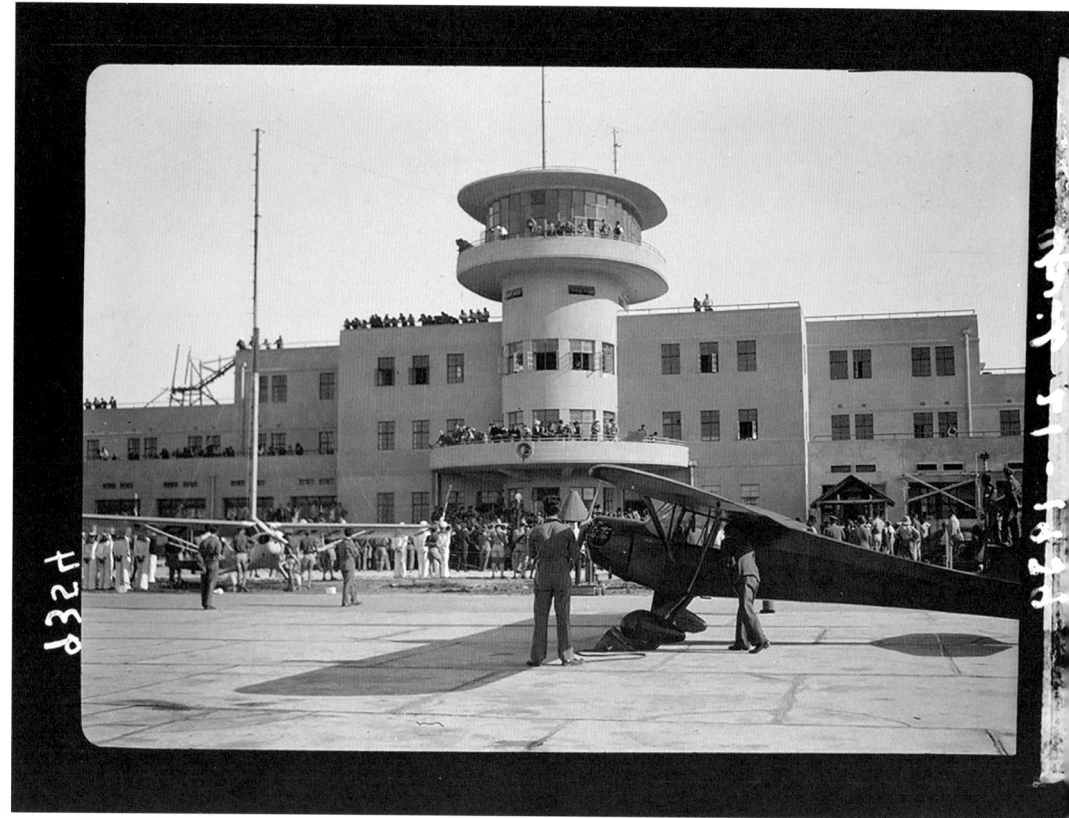

Left: Gaza Airport, 1935.

Right: Delivery of certificates from the Aviation School on April 21, 1939, at Lydda airport. The terminal building is in the background.

مطار غزة سنة 1935.

مطار اللد . نشاهد حفل تقديم الشهادات الصادرة عن مدرسة الطيران بتاريخ 21 أبريل سنة 1939. في الخلف يلاحظ بناية المطار.

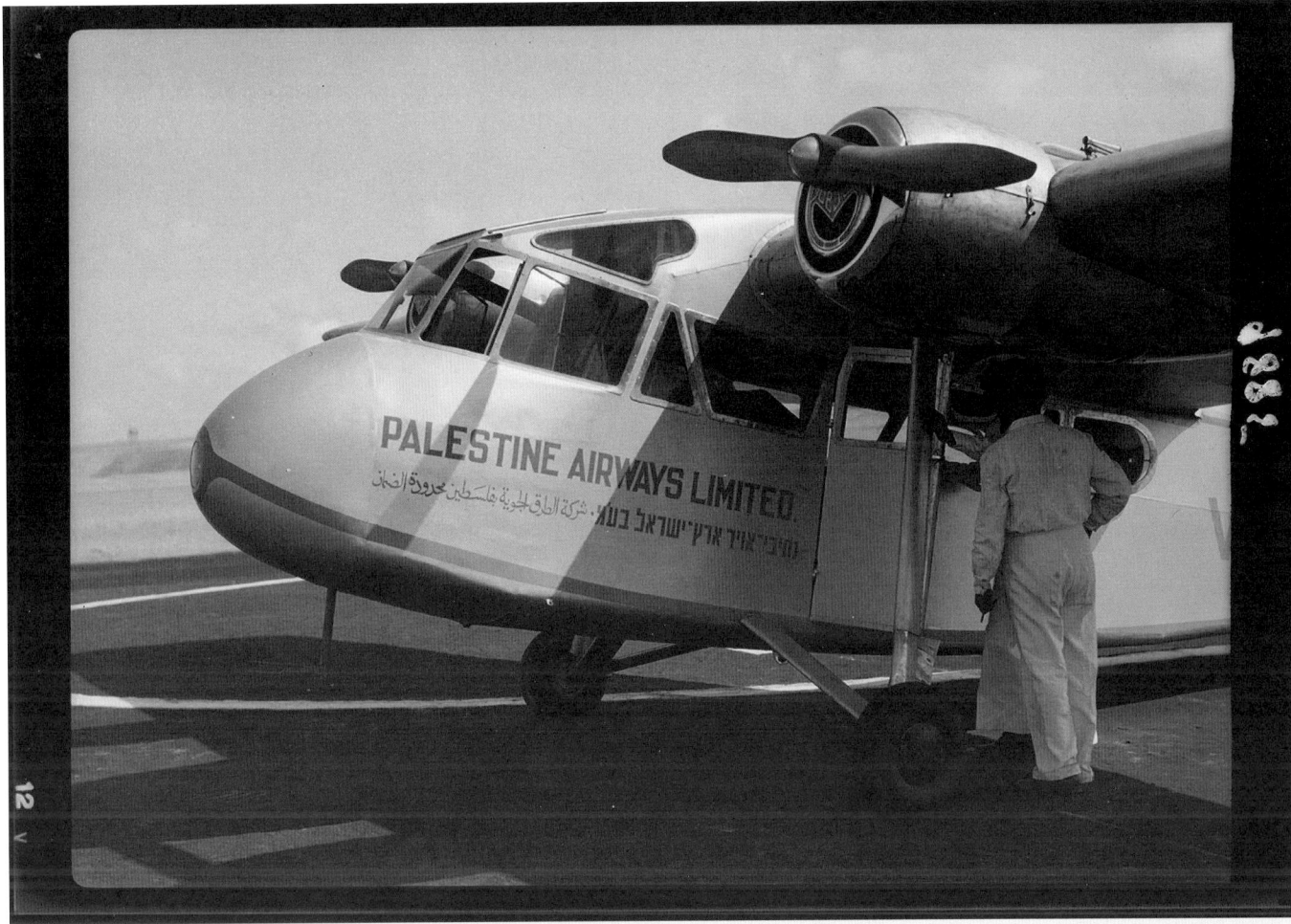

A Palestine Airways Ltd. airplane at the opening of the Lydda airport runway, with its branding in three languages, September 22, 1938.

حفل افتتاح مدرج مطار اللد . تشاهد طائرة تابعة لشركة خطوط الجو الفلسطينية المساهمة،وفد كتب عليها بثلاث لغات . الصورة ترجع إلى 22 سبتمبر 1938.

Left: Palestinian Post Office building, August 1920.

Right: Palestinian traffic police on duty, 1934–1939.

مكتب البريد الفلسطيني (قد يكون في القدس) أخذت في سنة 1920.

صورة لشرطي مرور في فلسطين وهو يؤدي عمله ، الصورة مؤرخة في الفترة من 1934 إلى 1939.

76

Left: The northern pier of the Palestine Potash Ltd. on the Dead Sea, 1934–1939.

Right: Palestine Potash Ltd. workers at the Ein Arus spring setting up a pipeline, 1934–1939.

موقع الشحن الشمالي لشركة البوتاس الفلسطينية المساهمة المحدودة في البحر الميت , تعود هذه الصورة الى الفترة 1943 إلى 1939.

صورة لعمال بشركة البوتاس الفلسطينية المساهمة في منبع عين عروس خلال علميات شق القناة . الصورة مؤرخة في الفترة 1934 إلى 1939.

A train at the Jerusalem railway station. 1898–1914.

قاطرة في محطة سكك الحديد في القدس 1898 إلى 1914.

The Railway Station, Jerusalem. 15 La Gare.

Left: The opening of the Jaffa–Jerusalem railway line, October 5, 1920.

Right: Jerusalem Train Station platform, 1898–1914.

الصورة في الأسفل حفل افتتاح خط القطار الذي يربط بين يافا والقدس بتاريخ 5 أكتوبر 1920.

الصورة تظهر رصيف محطة القطارات في القدس مؤرخة في الفترة بين 1898 إلى 1914.

89 Turkish Soldiers drilling in the Tower of Da[

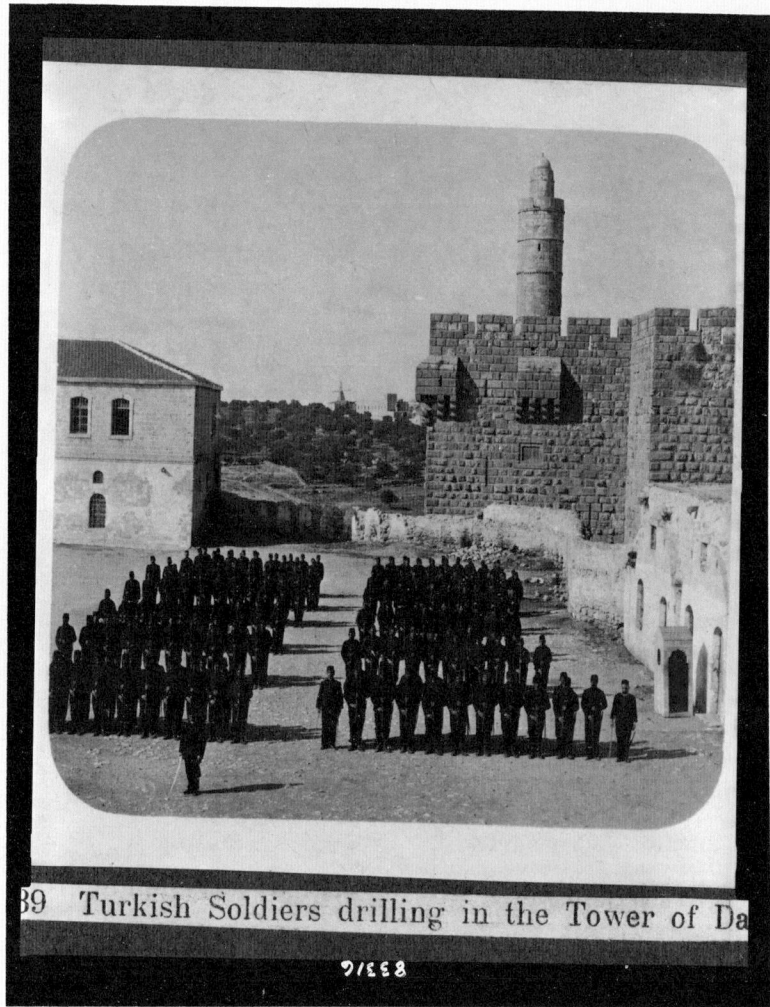

Left: Turkish soldiers training next to the Tower of David in Jerusalem, 1900–1914.
Right: A parade of British troops at Jaffa Gate in Jerusalem on December 11, 1917. The parade was held on the occasion of the start of the British Mandate on Palestine.

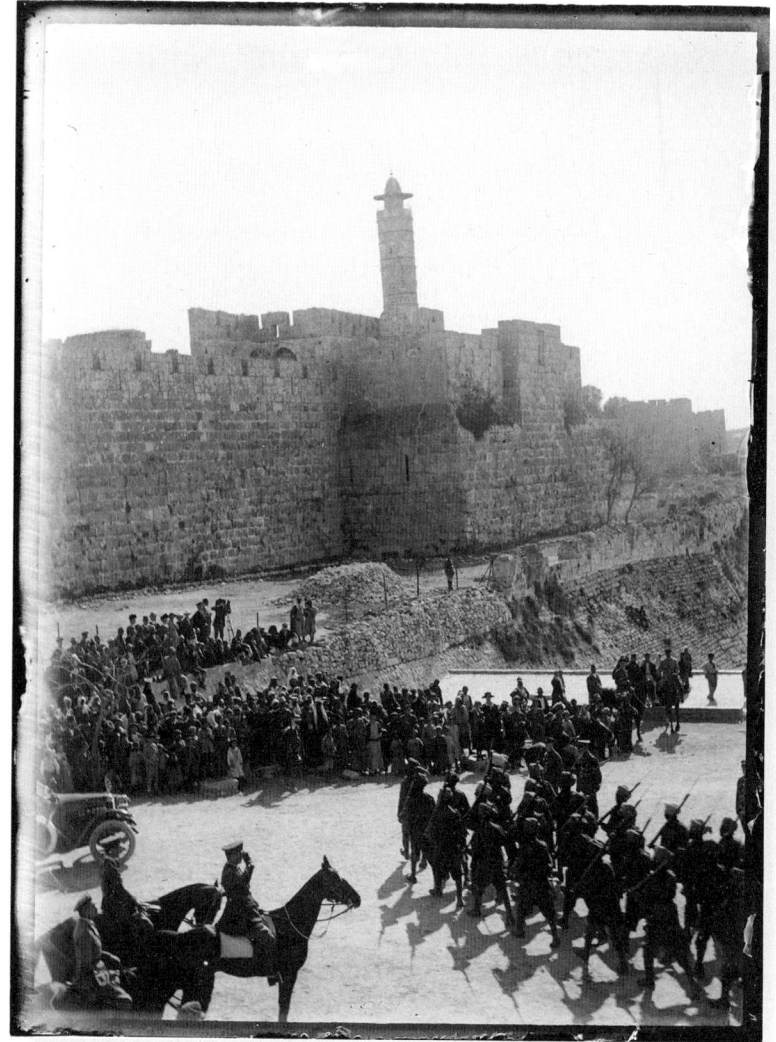

جنود أتراك يمارسون تدريباتهم بجانب برج داود في القدس . اخذت هذه الصورة خلال الفترة بين 1900 إلى 1914. أي خلال العهد العثماني.

استعراض للقوات البريطانية بتاريخ 11 ديسمبر 1917، أمام بوابة يافا في القدس، جرى بمناسبة بداية مرحلة الانتداب البريطاني في فلسطين.

From the photo album of a Haifa family showing General Allenby's entry into Jerusalem through Jaffa Gate on December 11, 1917.

صورتان من (البوم) عائلي لعائلة من حيفا تبين لحظة دخول الجنرال اللنبي في القدس من باب يافا بتاريخ 11 ديسمبر 1917.

Left to right: Lieutenant-Colonel T.E. Lawrence (Lawrence of Arabia, not in uniform), Emir Abdullah of Jordan, Sir Geoffrey Salmond (British Air Marshal), Sir Wyndham Deedes (Chief Secretary to the British Mandate High Commissioner), and Sir Herbert Samuel, June 30, 1920.

يظهر في الصورة (من اليسار الى اليمن) : العقيد الركن لورنس (لورنس العرب بلباس مدني)، ويليه الأمير عبد الله (الأردن) ، والسير جفري سلموند (مارشايل سلاح الجو البريطاني) والسير ويندلهام ديبس (السكرتير الرئيسي للندوب السامي للانتداب البريطاني) ، وأخير السير هيربرت سامويل . الترايخ 30 يونيو 1920.

The arrival of Sir Herbert Samuel as High Commissioner for Palestine. Left: Samuel is visiting some towns on July 10, 1920.

Right: Samuel is visiting the Tomb of Moses, 1920–1925.

صورتان للحظة لوصول السير هيربرت صامويل المندوب السامي في فلسطين. في الأيمن ونراه يزور بعض القرى بتاريخ 10 يونيو 1920.

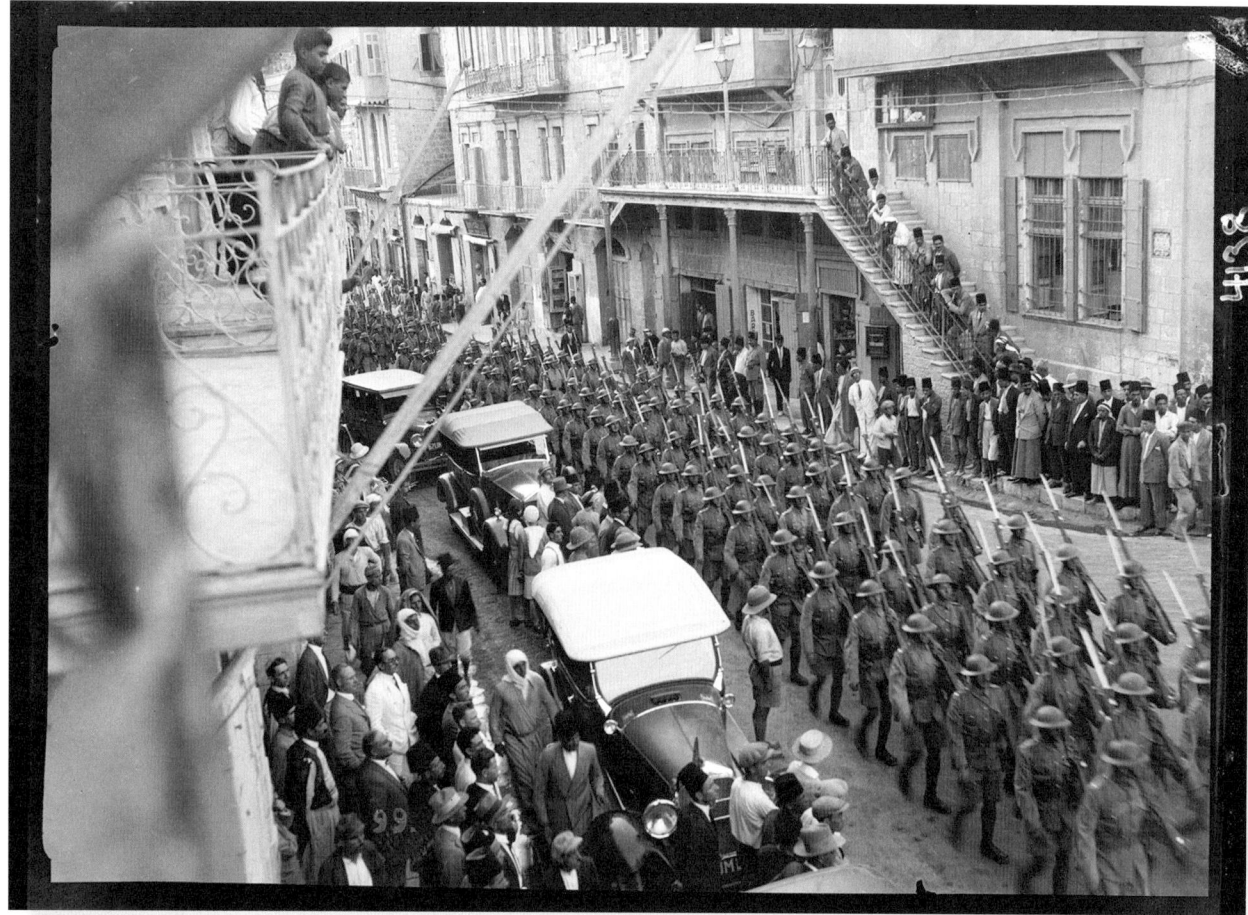

The 1929 riots. Left: The Jerusalem bazaar. On November 2, black flags appear in mourning for the Balfour Declaration with the inscription "Long Live Palestine."

Right: British troops taking to the streets of Jerusalem on August 23, 1931.

عدة صورة تبين الاحتجاجات التي جرت سنة 29. في الجانب الأيسر صورة للسوق الشعبي في القدس في يوم 2 نوفمبر. تظهر فيها اعلام سوداء حدادا على صدور وعد بلفور وقد كتب عليها (تحيى فلسطين).

وفى الصفحة التالية نرى متاجر مغلقة في يوم الحداد . احتجاجا لذلك الوعد المشئوم.

في الأسفل قوات بريطانية مجهزة بكل ما يلزم وهي تأخذ مواقعها في شوارع القدس بتاريخ 23 اغسطس 1931.

Shops are closed in a Day of Mourning to protest the declaration.

The very serious and growing unrest among the Palestinians arises from their absolute conviction that the present policy of the British Government is directed towards evicting them from their country in order to make it a national state for immigrant Jews... The Balfour Declaration was made without our being consulted and we cannot accept it as deciding our destinies.

"القلقُ البالغِ الخطورةِ والمتصاعدْ في صفوفِ الفلسطينيين، ناشيءٌ مِن قناعتِهِم المُطلقة، بأن السياسةَ الحاليةَ للحكومةِ البريطانية، مُوجّهة نَحو إجلائِهِم عن بلادِهِم بُغية جعلها دولة قومية للمهاجرين اليهود... إن تصريحَ وعد بلفور قد صدرَ دونَ استشارتِنا، وليسَ في وُسعِنا أن نرضى به لتقريرِ مصيرِنا".

رسالة مُوجّمة من تشرشل من الوفد العربي الذي توجه الى لندن للاعراب عن معارضته لشمل وعد بلفور ضمن شروط الانتداب البريطاني على فلسطين، بتاريخ 1921/10/24.

---

* Letter to Winston Churchill from the Arab delegation that traveled to London to oppose the inclusion of the Balfour Declaration in the terms of the British Mandate for Palestine, October 24, 1921.

The Arab protest delegation that traveled to London in December 1929. Among them, Raghib al-Nashashibi (second from left, an influential figure during both the Ottoman administration and the British Mandate), Fuad Abdul-Hadi (judge), Alfred Roch (representative of the Greek-Catholic Christian community of Jaffa), Sheikh Khatib, Amin al-Husseini (fourth, Grand Mufti of Jerusalem), Musa al-Husseini (fifth, Mayor of Jerusalem and leader of the Palestinian National Movement), and Awni Abdul-Hadi (one of the founders of Fatah and spokesman for the Arab Nationalist Movement in Palestine).

الوفد العربي الذي يمثل المتظاهرين يسافر الى لندن في ديسمبر 1929. من بين أعضاء الوفد رجب النشاشيبي (الثاني من اليسار)، من الشخصيات المؤثرة خلال الانتداب البريطاني ، والإدارة العثمانية)، فؤاد عبد الهادي (قاضي)، الفرد روش(ممثل الطائفة المسيحية اليونانية الكاثوليكية في يافا)، الشيخ خطيب، أمين الحسيني (رابع مفتي كبير لمدينة القدس)، وعوني عبد الهادي (احد مؤسسو حركة فتح وناطق باسم الحركة القومية العربية في فلسطين).

We, the representatives of the Palestine Arab Nation in the Fifth Palestine Arab Congress, held at Nablus, pledge ourselves to God, history, and the Nation that we shall continue our endeavors for the independence of our country, and for achieving Arab unity by all legal methods, and that we shall not accept the establishing of a Jewish National Home … *

---

* Fifth Arab Congress of Palestine, held in Nablus in August 1922. Cited in A. W. Kayyali, *Palestine: A Modern History* (London: Croom Helm, 1978).

"نحنُ مُمثلي الشعب العربي الفلسطيني في المؤتمر العربي الفلسطيني الخامس المعقود في نابلس، نتعهد أمامَ الله والتاريخ والشعب على أن نستمرَ في جهودنا الرامية إلى إستقلال بلادنا وتحقيق الوحدة العربية بجميع الوسائل المشروعة، وسوفَ لا نقبلُ بإقامةِ وطنٍ قوميٍ يهودي...".

المؤتمر العربي الخامس لفلسطين، المنعقد في نابلس،اغسطس آب 1922.

المرجع:تاريخ فلسطين الحديث د.عبدالوهاب الكيالي، دار النشر بوسفورو،مدريد2014.

Palestinian Conference prior to the Fourth Palestinian Delegation to London, March 1930. In the front row, from left to right: Awni Abdul-Hadi, Haj Amin al-Husseini, Musa Kazim al-Husseini, Raghib al-Nashashibi, and Alfred Roch.

المشاركون في الاجتماع التحضيري لتشكيل الوفد الفلسطيني الرابع لزيارة لندن، في مارس 1930. في الصف الأول نشاهد من اليسار إلى اليمين: عوني عبد الهادي، والحاج أمين الحسيني، وموسى قاسم الحسيني، ورجب النشاشيبي وأخير الفرد وش.

Members of the Arab Higher Committee. Front row, left to right: Raghib al-Nashashibi, Chairman of the Defense Party; Haj Amin al-Husseini, Grand Mufti and Chairman of the Committee; Ahmed Hilmi Pasha, General Director of the Arab Bank of Jerusalem; Abdul Latif Bey al-Salah, chairman of the Arab Nationalist Party; and Alfred Roch, influential landowner.

Right: Grand Mufti Amin al-Husseini after giving a statement to the Royal Commission for Palestine. 1937.

اللجنة العربية العليا من اليسار إلى اليمين ابتداء من الصف الأول: رجب بيك النشاشيبي رئيس حزب الدفاع، الحاج أمين الحسيني (المفتي الأكبر للقدس) ورئيس اللجنة، أحمد حلمي باشا المدير العام للبنك العربي في القدس وعبد اللطيف بيك الصلاح رئيس الحزب القومي العربي والسير الفريد روش الاقطاعي المتنفذ.

The Great Revolt of 1936–1937. The inhabitants of Abu Gosh, a town west of Jerusalem, take an oath of allegiance to the Arab Higher Committee in April 1936.

صورتان إضافيتان من الاحتجاجات الكبرى التي جرت سنة 1936. سكان منطقة أبو غوش القرية من القدس يقسمون يمين الولاء والبيعة للجنة العربية العليا ، في أبريل سنة 1936.

British engineers standing in front of the rubble of houses blown up with dynamite in Jaffa during the Arab protests in the summer of 1936.

صورتان التقطتا في صيف سنة 1936 خلال الاحتجاجات العربية. مساكن مدمرة بالديناميت في يافا، الصورة تظهر مهندسون بريطانيون امام ما تبقى من المساكن المدمرة.

Arab homes destroyed by the British military during the 1936 revolt. Left: Former inhabitants searching for belongings in the rubble of their home in Lydda.

Right: Demolished houses in Halhul in southern Palestine.

صورتان ثانيتان للبيوت العربية المنسوفة بآمر عسكري بريطاني خلال المظاهرات التي جرت سنة 1936. يظهر سكان هذه المساكن يفتشون بين الانقاض في مدينة اللد . إلى اليمين المزيد من انقاض بيوت آخرى نسفت في حلحول جنوب فلسطين.

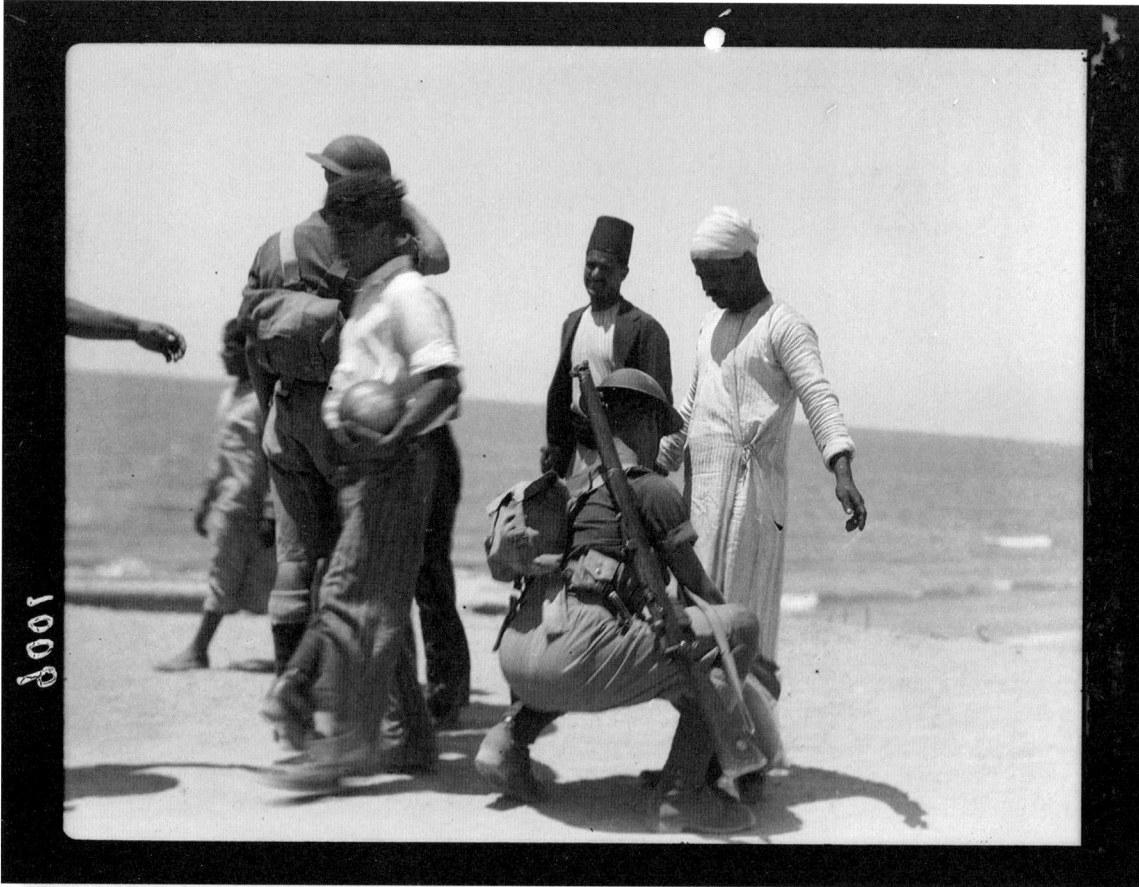

Left: British soldiers frisk Jaffa residents for weapons during the 1936 riots.

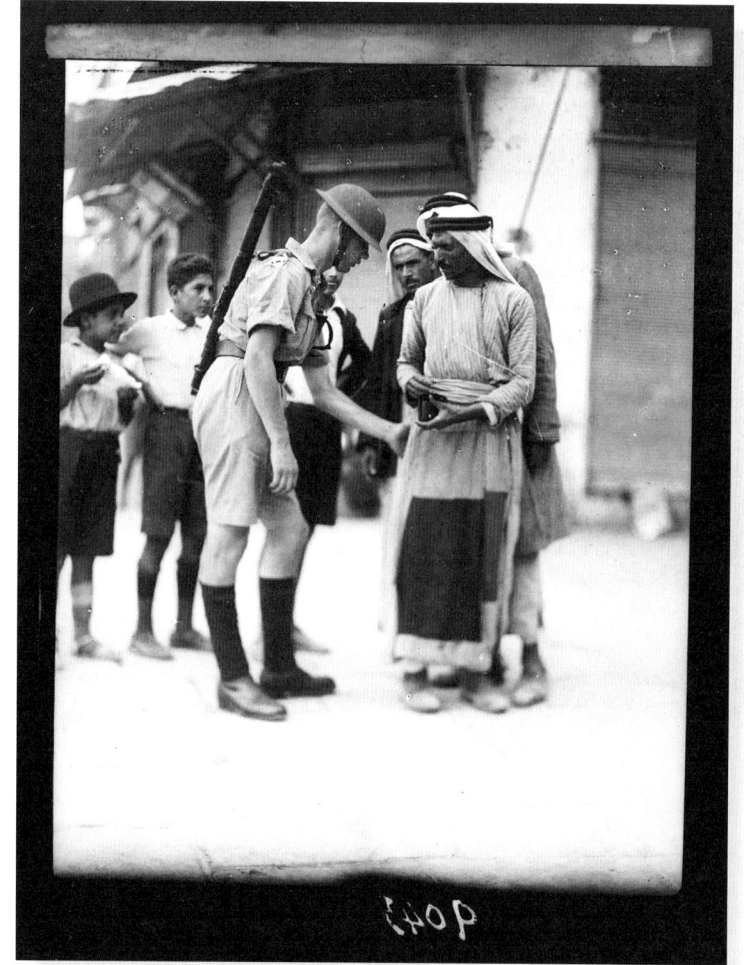

Right: Jerusalem residents being frisked at the Jaffa Gate.

الصورة اليسرى تظهر عمليات تفتيش عن سلاح بحوزة سكان يافا خلال المظاهرات في صيف سنة 1936. وفي الصورة اليمنى المزيد من المواطنين الفلسطينيين يتعرضون للتفتيش،هذه المرة في القدس، عند بوابة يافا.

The end of the general strike, May 1936–July 1937. The strike caused almost total economic and commercial paralysis throughout Palestine.
Left: The leader of the boatmen and stevedores as they prepare to resume work in Jaffa.

Right: The first boat to unload cargo from a ship after the end of the general strike in Jaffa.

اللحظتان سجلتا في نهاية الإضراب العام الذي بدأ في مايو 1936 وانتهى في يوليو 1937 . لقيت الدعوة لذلك الإضراب استجابة واسعة في معظم المناطق الفلسطينية وفي كافة القطاعات مما أدى إلى شلل شبه كلي لكافة النشاطات الاقتصادية والتجارية.

في الصورة اليسرى نشاهد زعيم قطاع تسيير القوارب والشحن خلال استعداده لاستئناف العمل في يافا.وفي الأيمن أول قارب يفرغ حمولته من السلع التي نقلت في باخرة تجارية بعد انتهاء الإضراب في ميناء يافا.

Riots in Hebron, 1938. Left: The Bank of Hebron burned by Arab rebels.

Right: The Post Office after the August 19 attack.

مشهد من الاضطرابات في الخليل سنة 1938. وفي الأعلى بنك الخليل وقد شبت فيه النيران التي أشعلها المتمردون العرب. وفي الصورة اليمنى نشاهد مكتب البريد بعد تعرضه للهجوم في 19 اغسطس.

Left: Rocks placed by Arab groups blocking the passage of police and military vehicles on the Hebron highway, August 19, 1938.

Right: Arabs being frisked for weapons at the Jerusalem bus station on Jaffa Road, during the 1938 riots.

مجموعات من العرب تضع المتاريس لاعتراض سيارات الأمن والعسكر على الطريق الى مدينة الخليل، بتاريخ. 19 أغسطس 1938.

عمليات تفتيش في محطة الحافلات والمتوجمة إلى القدس من يافا بحثا عن اسلحة لدى السكان العرب، وذلك خلال أعمال الشغب التي شهدتها فلسطين سنة 1938.

Palestinian women took an active part in the protests during the British Mandate. In this photograph, a delegation of Palestinian women are pictured in front of the High Commissioner's residence in Jerusalem. The delegation came together to protest British brutality during the riots of 1929.

Second from the left is the Palestinian feminist leader Matiel Moghannam, author of *The Arab Woman and the Palestine Problem* (London: H. Joseph, 1937). The First Arab Women's Conference took place in Jerusalem, October 26–29, 1929. Some of the activists who participated in this conference were Andalib al-Amad, Milia Sakakini, Ni'mati al-Alami, Katrin Siksik from Jerusalem, Adele Azar from Jafa, Mariam Khalil and Sathij Nassar from Haifa, and Nabiha Mansi and Ruqaya al-Karmin from Acre. *

---

* Walid Khalidi, *Before Their Diaspora: A Photographic History of the Palestinians, 1876–1948* (Beirut: Institute for Palestine Studies, 2010).

شاركت النساء الفلسطينيات -من المسيحيات والمسلمات- بشكل فعال في الاحتجاجات خلال مرحلة الانتداب البريطاني.

نشاهد في الصورة وفدا من النساء الفلسطينيات أمام مقر المندوب السامي البريطاني في القدس. الوفد النسائي تجمع للاحتجاج

على الممارسات القمعية البريطانية خلال الاحتجاجات التي شهدتها البلاد سنة 1929.

نشاهد في الصورة الثانية من اليسار السيدة الفلسطينية ماتييل مغنم وهي من المدافعات عن المساواة بين الرجل والمرأة،

مؤلفة كتاب المرأة العربية والقضية الفلسطينية الذي صدر في لندن سنة 1937 عن دار نشر ش. جوزيف.

المؤتمر الأول للمرأة العربية عقد في القدس خلال الفترة 26 إلى 29 أكتوبر سنة 1929.

من بين المشاركات في ذلك المؤتمر الناشطات: عنداليب العمد ميليا السكاكيني، ونعيمة العلمي، والمقدسية كارتين سيكسيك،

وعديل الزار من يافا ، ومريم خليل، وساتيج ناصر من حيفا، ونبيلة المنسي ,رقية الكرملي من عكا.

96

On October 12, 1938, the Palestinian delegation departed from Lydda to participate in the First Conference of Arab Women in Cairo, which took place October 15–18.

The central theme of the conference was support for Palestine, and it was attended by delegations from Syria, Egypt, Iraq, Lebanon, and Iran. The Palestinian delegation was the largest (27 participants).

The conference supported the Palestinian revolution, demanded the release of prisoners, and called for a boycott of British products. It also supported Palestinian demands for the cancellation of the Balfour Declaration, the halting of Jewish immigration, and the cessation of the illegal transfer of Arab lands to Jews. It condemned the brutal repression by the British police of the Palestinian population.*

تاريخ 12 أكتوبر 1938 غادر الوفد الفلسطيني مطار اللّد للمشاركة في مؤتمر المرأة العربية الأول الذي عقد في القاهرة خلال الفترة

من 15 ألى 18 اكتوبر من السنة المذكورة . الموضوع الرئيسي في ذلك المؤتمر كان دعم نضال الشعب الفلسطيني، شاركت في المؤتمر

وفود من سوريا والعراق ومصر ولبنان وإيران بالإضافة للوفد الفلسطيني الأكثر عددا (27) سيدة . اتخذ المؤتمر قرارات مساندة للثور

ة الفلسطينية وطالب بإطلاق سراح السجناء وحث على مقاطعة السلع البريطانية. كما أعلن تأييده لمطلب الشعب الفلسطيني المتعلق

بإلغاء وعد بلفور، ووقف الهجرة اليهودية والتوقف عن نقل ملكية الأراضي العربية بطرق غير مشروعة للمهاجرين اليهود وأخيرا استنكر

الأعمال القمعية للشرطة البريطانية ضد الفلسطينيين.

---

* Kayyali, *Palestine: A Modern History*

Members of the Commission of Inquiry for Palestine accompanied by Arab representatives
during their visit to Al-Aqsa Mosque in Jerusalem in March 1946.

صورتان لأعضاء لجنة التحقيق المتعلقة بفلسطين، برفقة ممثلين عرب خلال الزيارة التي قامت بها اللجنة الى مسجد الأقصى في القدس في شهر مارس 1946.

From the Haifa Midawwar family album, a Christian family that lost all of its property in 1948 except for one small apartment.

صور من البوم عائلة المدور من حيفا . عائلة مسيحية خسرت كافة ممتلكاتها باستثناء شقة صغيرة سنة 1948.

Left: Amis Kusta Midawwar.

أميس كوستا مدور (في الدائرة كعلامة) كما يظهر في الصورة ذات الإطار.

A family portrait of Bishara Midawwar and his wife and children, taken in Canada.

صورة لعائلة المدور أخذت في كندا . بشارة مدور مع زوجته وأبناءه.

The Khoury building in Haifa, which was later taken over by the Palestinian Railway Company. The building was a meeting point for the Palestinian resistance, for which it was burned down by Haganah militias.

عمارة عائلة الخوري في حيفا، والتي اصبحت فيما بعد مكاتب لشركة القطارات الفلسطينية. كانت هذه العمارة ملتقى للثوار الفلسطينيين، لذا تعرضت للحرق من قبل عصابة الهغنا.

The men of the Midawwar family. Photograph taken at the Haifa casino. Second from the left in the light-colored suit is Sami Abyad, the last person to be killed in the assault on Haifa.

رجال من عائلة المدور. الصورة اخذت في كازينو حيفا ، سامي عبيد، الثاني من اليسار بدله فاتحة هو أخر ضحية سقطت خلال اجتياح حيفا.

Among the photographs in the Midawwar family album were several portraits of Alexia Khoury in evening dress, dated 1930.

عائلة العيسي. من بين صور الألبوم العائلي لبيت المدور نجد عدة صور شخصية لأفراد من عائلة الخوري ، تعرفنا على اسم العيسى خوري أربع صور شخصية بملابس السهرة تعود هذه الصور الى 1930.

Left: Alexia's mother sitting in an armchair, 1930s.

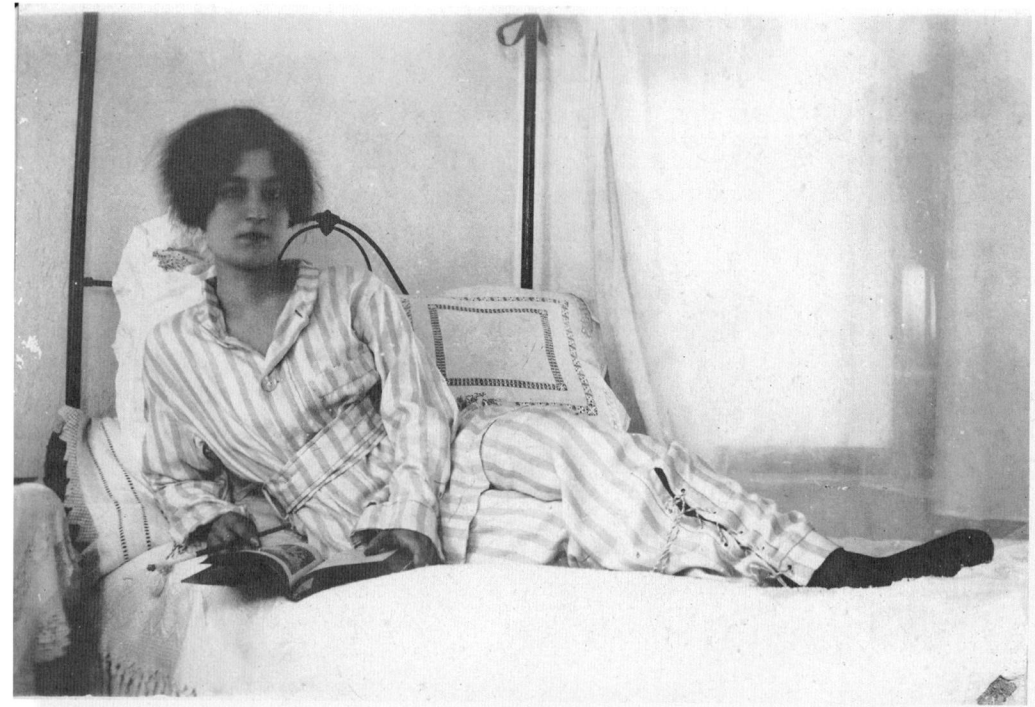

Right: A woman in pajamas lying on the bed, 1930s.

صورة شخصية لوالدة الكيسا، وهي جالسة في اريكة . عقد الثلاثينات. الى جانبها نشاهد سيدة ترتدي البيجاما مضطجعة على السرير. عقد الثلاثينات.

A group of friends in the Palestinian countryside, 1930s.

في الأسفل مجموعة من الأصدقاء في الريف عقد الثلاثينات.

From the album of the Abyad family of Haifa: A young girl outside her family home in Haifa.

صورة من الألبوم العائلي لعائلة أبيض من مدينة حيفا.

صورة لفتاة يانعة خارج البيت العائلي في مدينة حيفا.

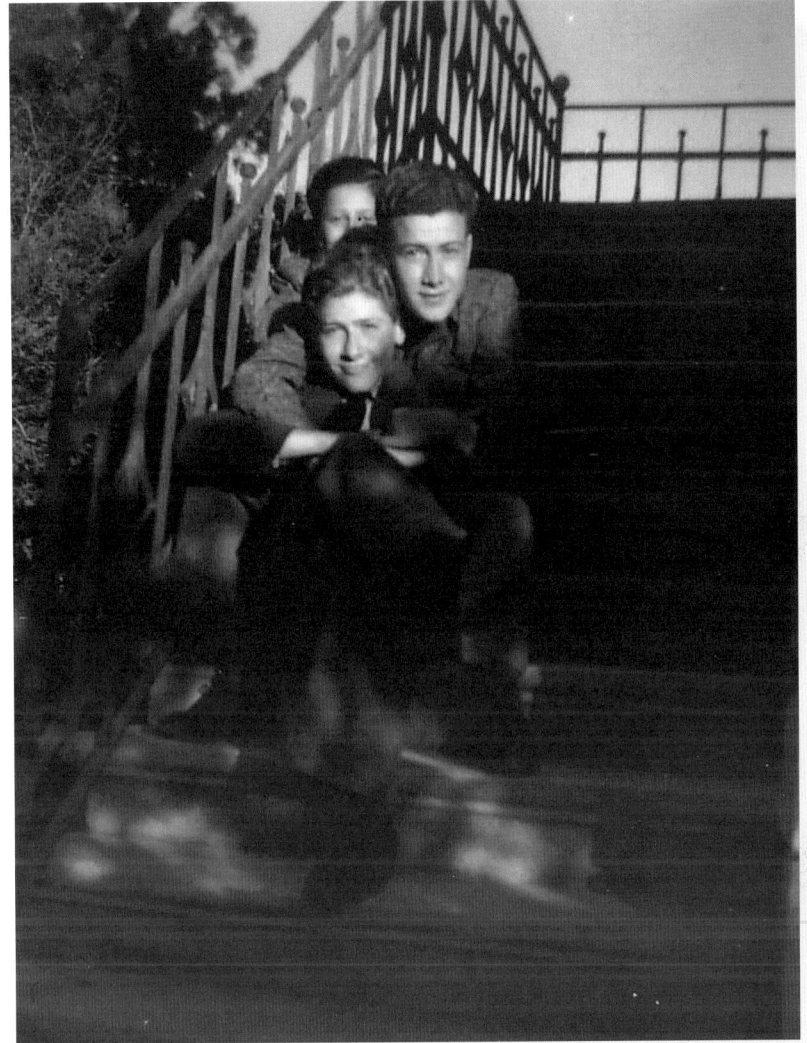

Left: Abyad family members on the stairs outside their home. Right: Renée Germain with Anis and Raymonde.

صورة أخرى لعدد من أفراد العائلة على الدرج في مدخل البيت. ريني جرماين ، أبيض برفقة انيس رايموند

The Mansour family of Haifa. Left: Elias Hanna Mansour, 1947.

Right (top): A group of friends: Atif, Jubran, Zaki, Elias Mansour (third from the right), Kareem, Issa, and Jameel. Right (bottom): Basila Issa, Elias Mansour (second from left), Kareem, and others in the village of Jish.

صورة عائلية لعائلة منصور   صورة للسيد إلياس حنا منصور سنة 1947. الى اليسار.

باسيلا عيسى، والياس منصور، وكريم وآخرين في الصرة السفلية.

Photographs taken by Amal Jaber, a teacher at the Saint Gabriel School, in Carmel Station, Haifa, before 1948.

صورة اخذت من قبل أمل جابر، استاذة في مدرسة سان جبريل، في محطة الكرمل (حيفا) قبل سنة 1948.

Left: Students from Saint Gabriel School on the day of their First Communion. Right: Family members standing with the priest.

عدة طلبة من مدرسة سانت جبريل بمناسبة الاحتفال بتعميدهم الأول. وفي اليمين عائلات الطلاب برفقة القسيس.

Education data for Palestine, 1927

Total students: 130,000, out of a population of 1,238,000.
School-age children: 85 percent of children in cities and 63 percent in rural areas. School-age girls: 60 percent enrolled in cities and 7.5 percent in rural areas. There were 827 Arab schools in the academic year 1945–46, of which 514 were government schools, 131 were Islamic schools, and 182 were Church-affiliated schools. At the beginning of the 1947–48 academic year, there were 12 Arab comprehensive secondary schools in Palestine and 20 offering noncomprehensive courses.

The existing educational institutions in the Arab countries, such as those of Cairo, Alexandria, Beirut, Damascus, and Baghdad, began to include Palestinian children, which according to the 1948 census amounted to 3 students in Syrian institutes, 15 in Iraq, 416 in Lebanon, and 631 in Egypt.[*]

معلومات عن التعليم المدرسي في فلسطين سنة 1927

العد الاجمالي للطلاب: 130.000 من عدد سكان إجمالي قدره 1.238.000 نسمة.

طلاب من الذكور في سن الدراسة: نسبة 85% من الأطفال من سكان المدن و 63% من المناطق الريفية.

طلبات من الاناث في سنة الدراسة: 60% من بنات سكان المدن و 7,5% من المناطق الريفية.

عدد المدارس العربية خلال السنة الدراسية 1945-1946 بلغ 827 مدرسة .منها 514 مدرسة حكومية، و131 مدرسة إسلامية و 182 مدرسه مسيحية. وفي مطلع النسة الدراسية 1947-1948 كان يتواجد في فلسطين 12 مدرسة ثانونية عربية كاملة الفصول، و20 مدرسة تحتوي على بعض الفصول غير متكاملة.

معاهد ومراكز التعليم المتواجدة في الدول العربية كالقاهرة، والإسكندرية وبيروت، ودمشق ، وبغداد، بدأت تستقطب اعداد غير قليلة من أبناء فلسطين، وطبقا للإحصائيات سنة 1948 وثل العدد 3 طلبة في المعاهد السورية، و15 في العراق، و416 في لبنان، و631 في مصر.

* 'Abd Al-Rahman Yaghi, "Factores determinantes del renacimiento cultural palestino," *Cuadernos de Almenara*, no 7 (Madrid: Editorial CantArabia, 1993).

Passports of members of the the al-Farra family, a Christian family from Haifa, issued in Jerusalem in 1944 under the British Mandate.

ألبوم عائلة الفرا في حيفا عائلة مسيحية. المصور اميلي الفرا والصورة أخذت بكميرا لايكا هدية من والد المصور.

The al-Farra family photo album.

Right: A family photograph taken during a trip to the Qadisha Caves in Lebanon, 1935.

عدة صفحات من جواز سفر عائلي صدر في القدس سنة 1944 خلال عهد الانتداب البريطاني.

صورة عائلية أخذت خلال رحلة إلى مغارة قادس في لبنان سنة 1935.

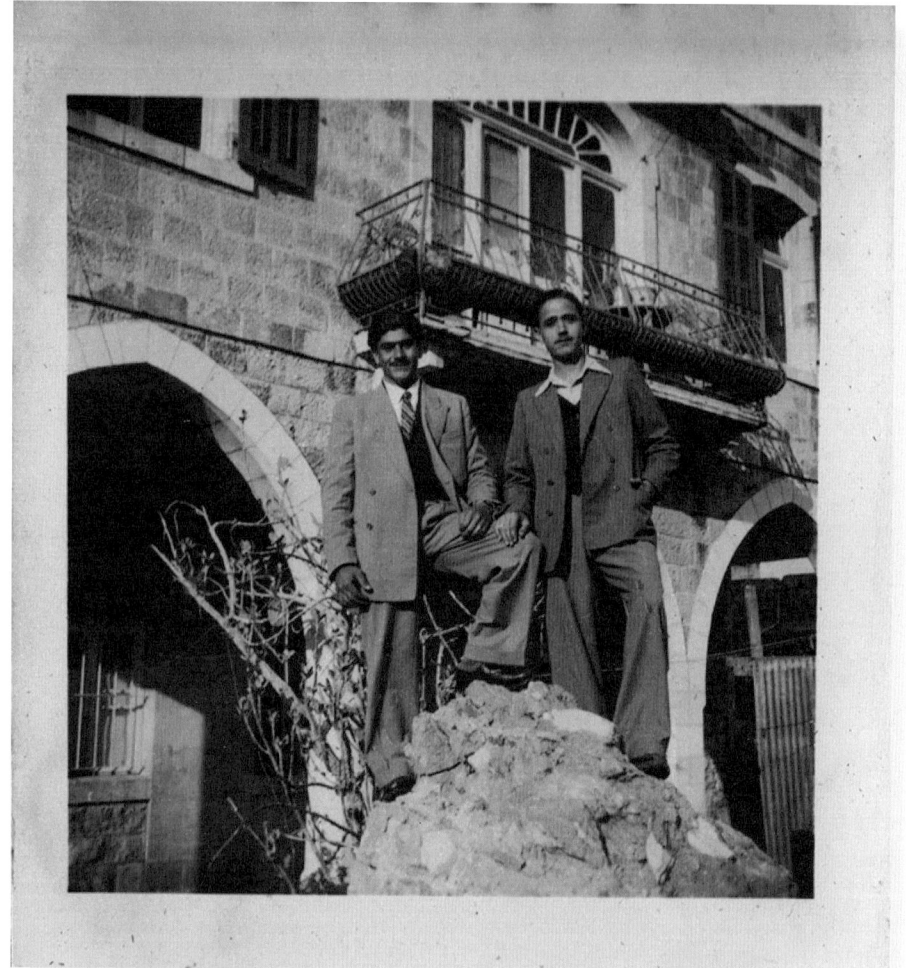

Left: Emile al-Farra (left) with a group of friends at Stella Maris Monastery on Mount Carmel, Haifa.

Right: Emile al-Farra (left), with a friend in King George V School, Haifa, 1947.

اميلي عفارة واقفا وهو (الأول من اليسار) برفقة مجموعة من الأصدقاء في دير استيلا ماريس في جبل الكرمل (حيفا).

صورة لأميلي عفارة مع أحد الأصدقاء في مدرسة الملك جورج الخامس في حيفا 1947.

Left: Emile Effara (second from right) with friends on April 21, 1948, one day before the fall of Haifa.

Right: "The Year of Snow," early 1950s. Haifa residents were able to visit neighboring villages because Israeli soldiers left their positions and the curfew was partially lifted.

اميلي الفرا من جديد (الثاني من اليمين) برفقة أصدقاء في سيارة بتاريخ 21/ أبريل 1948، يوم واحد قبل سقوط مدينة حيفا.

"سنة الثلجة" مطلع سنة 1950. سكان حيفا استطاعوا زيارة القرى المجاورة لأن الجنود الإسرائيليين غادروا مواقعهم ورُفع حظر التجول جزئيا بسبب الثلج المتساقط.

Left: During the siege and bombardment of Haifa in April 1948, many families took refuge in their country homes. The al-Farra family went to the Stella Maris Monastery on Mount Carmel. They stayed there for two years; when they returned to Haifa, their home was in the hands of a Jewish family.

Right: Members of the al-Farra family at the entrance to the Stella Maris Monastery on Mount Carmel, Haifa.

في الصورة العلوية بعض أفراد عائلة عفارة عند مدخل دير استيا ماريس في جبل الكرمل بحيفا.

التجأت الكثير من العائلات إلى مزارعها في الريف ، أفراد عائلة عفارة التجئوا إلى الدير الموجود في جبل الكرمل .
في هذا المكان طوال سنتين ، وعندما عادوا إلى حيفا وجدوا بيتهم محتلا من قبل عائلة يهودية.

الى اليمن عائلة عفارة على بوابة دير استيلا ماريس في جبل الكرمل

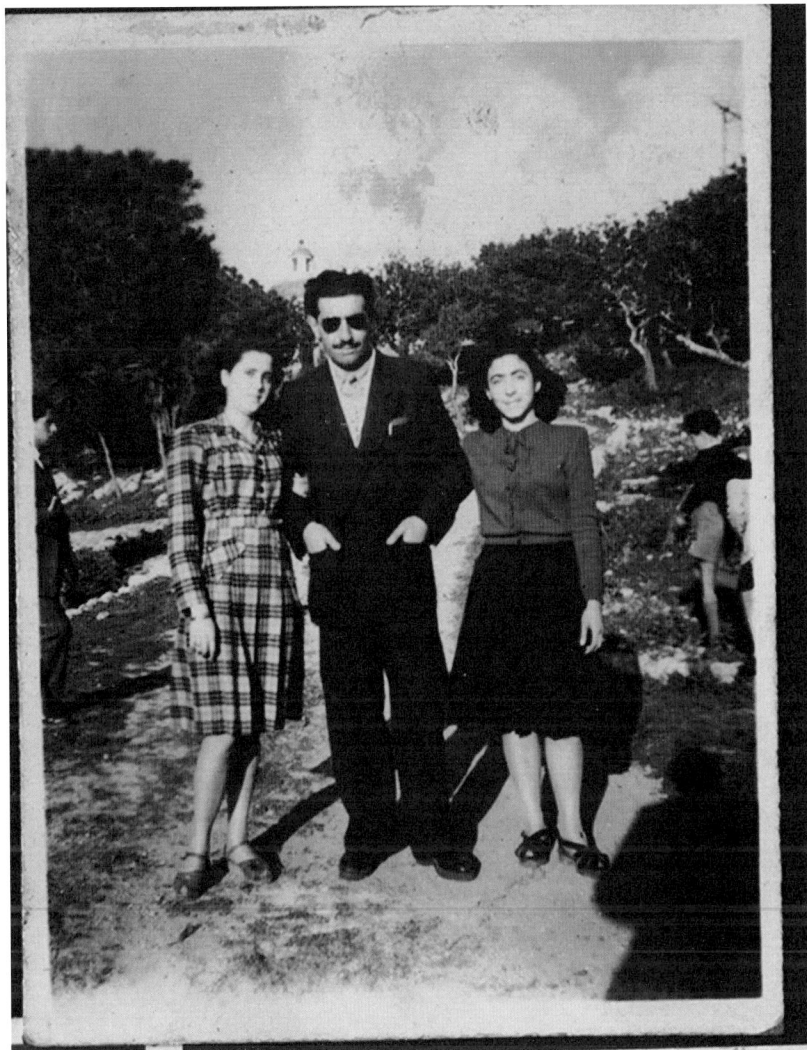

From the al-Farra family album.

صورتان ثانيتان من ألبوم عائلة الفرا.

Studio portraits of Christian children on Palm Sunday.

من صور الاستوديو لأطفال لعائلات مسيحية يوم عيد الاغصان.

The wedding picture of Farid and Margaret Sa'ad. July 1938.

صورة من عرس فريد سعد ومارغاريت في يوليو 1938.

Left: Bishop Gregorio Haijar of the Greek Catholic Church meets with school principals and teachers, 1934.

Right: Two imams from Al-Aqsa Mosque and Archimandrite Basileus Qassis, 1945.

لقاء بين بطرك الكنيسة – الإغريقية – الكاثوليكية (جريجوريو حجار) مع مدراء ومعلمي المدارس سنة 1934.

في الصورة الى اليمين اثنان من أئمة المسجد الأقصى مع البطريارك باسيليوس قصيص 1945.

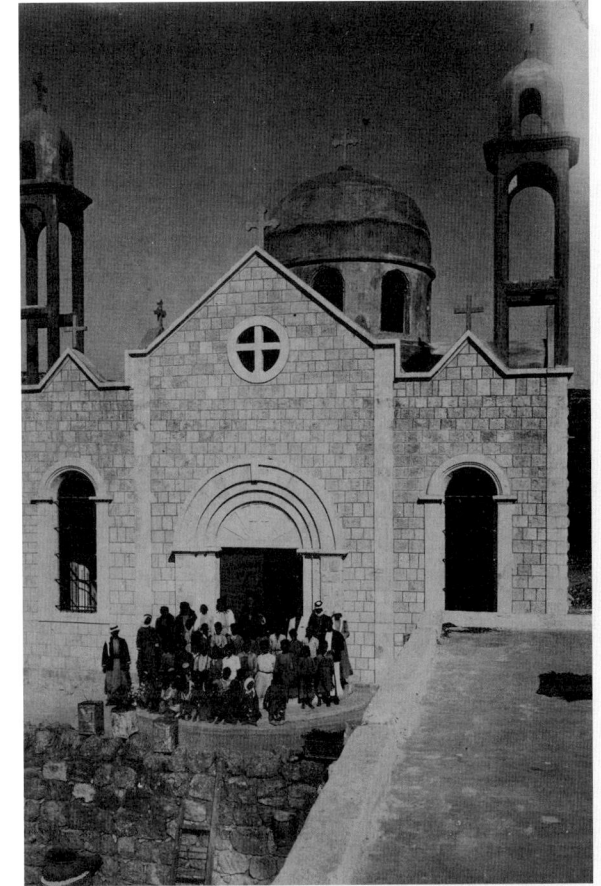

Left: A procession of children in Nazareth at the funeral of Bishop Gregorio Haijar, who was noted for his Arab nationalist activism, 1940.

Right: Ma'aloul Church, near Nazareth. The town Ma'aloul, whose residents were Muslim and Christian, was destroyed in 1948; only the two churches and a mosque remain. Each Easter Sunday, both Christian and Muslim former residents visit their respective places of worship.

نشاهد استعرضا لشباب القرية في جنازة زعيم الكنسية غريغوريو حجار وهو شخصية معروفة بنشاطه دفاعا عن القومية العربية. سنة 1940.

كنسية معلول بالقرب من الناصرة بلدة يقطنها مسلمون ومسيحيون دمرت سنة 1948. لم يبق فيها سوى كنيستين ومسجد. يقوم سكان هذه القرية القدماء من المسلمين والمسحيين سنويا بالعودة الى الكنيسة لإحياء عيد الفصح.

Left: Haifa Municipal Council (Arabs, Jews, and British nationals). Mayor Hassan Shukry stands in the center and is wearing a tarbush; Ibrahim Sahyun is third from the right (also wearing a tarbush). David Cohen stands in the second row and is wearing glasses and a bow tie.

Right: Some staff of Haifa Islamic School, 1945.

الصورة المجلس البلدي لمدينة حيفا يتألف من (عرب ويهود وبريطانيون) . عميد البلدية حسن شكري في الوسط يلبس
طربوشا . الرجل الثالث من اليمين بطربوش إبراهيم صهيون، ودافيد كوهين بنظارات وربطة عنق.

في الصورة اليمنى بعض العاملين في المدرسة الإسلامية بحيفا سنة 1945.

Left: Three young people in a small boat; photograph taken in a professional studio, August 15, 1938.

Right: Students and teachers from the Salesian Schools of Haifa in a theater performance.

صورة لثلاثة شباب في استوديو تصوير اقيم في قارب. 15 اغسطس سنة 1938.

عرض مسرحي بمشاركة طلبة ومدرسين في مدرسة جماعة الساليسيانيوس في حيفا.

المجموعة البابوية البيتجالية ١٩٥٢

Various Boy Scout troupes. The Scout Movement arrived in Palestine in 1912. Left (bottom): Beit Yala Scout Group. 1953.

Right (bottom): From the Saqqa family album (Bethlehem).

صور لعدة فرق من الكشافة مجهولة الهوية . بدأت حركة الكشافة الى فلسطين سنة 1912.

A group of scouts. From the Saqqa family album (Bethlehem).

صور لفرق الكشافة من البوم عائلة السقا في بيت لحم. في الصفحة السابقة المجموعة السفلية الى اليمن، جزء من نفس الألبوم.

Left: The inscription reads "Guardians of Beit Yala. 1936–1939." From the Saqqa family album (Bethlehem)

Right: Grandfather and grandson (Kattan family) during a visit to Bethlehem. From the Kattan family album.

إلى اليمن الجد وحفيده من عائلة كتان خلال زيارة الى بيت لحم

Palestinian soccer teams. On this page, the first Bethlehem football team in 1932. From the Saqqa family album.

صورة لفرق كرة القدم في بيت لحم سنة 1932 من الألبوم الخاص بعائلة السقا.

The Haifa Salesians soccer team in 1940. The Palestinian flag can be seen on the shirts. The school was shut down by the British authorities in 1941.

فريق مدرسة جماعة الساليسان في حيفا . فازوا في الدوري الفلسطيني سنة 1940 على القميص نشاهد علم فلسطين . اغلقت هذه المدرسة من قبل البريطانيون سنة 1941. فريق جماعة السالسيان.

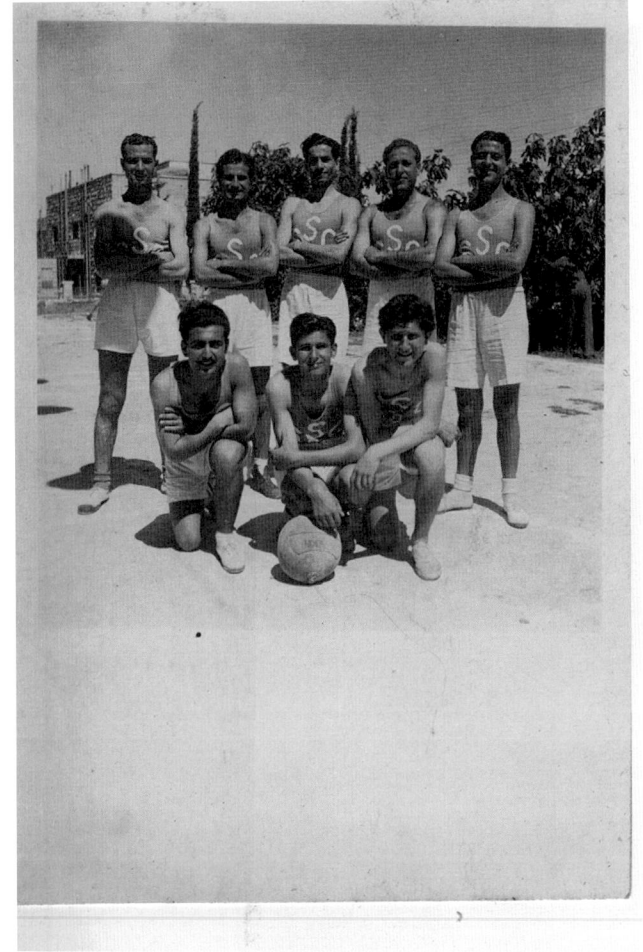

Left: The Haifa Salesians team. Elias Mansur, the father of Johnny Mansour (one of the contributors to this book) appears third from the right, 1940.

Right: The basketball team from the same school, 1940.

إلى اليسار صورة أخرى لفريق كرة القدم التابع لجماعة السيليسيانوس بمدينة حيفا . الشخص الظاهر في الصورة الثالث من اليمين هو إلياس منصور ، والد جوني منصور صاحب هذه المجموعة من الصور .

إلى اليسار صورة اخرى لفريق الساليسيان لكرة القدم في حيفا. الشخص الثالث من اليمين هو الياس منصور (والد جوني) صاحب هذه المجموعة من الصور سنة 1940.

Students of the Haifa Carmelite school, 1940.

طلبة مدرسة الراهبات كارميلتياس بمدينة حيفا (بنات وأولاد). 1940.

Several photographs from the album of Olga Kattan, a student at Schmidt's Girls College in Jerusalem.

Left: In the courtyard of Olga Kattan's boarding school. The seven-year-old Olga is standing (front row, fourth from left) with her classmates, Mother Árab, and Father Sonen, the school principal.

Right: Students with an Arab and a Yugoslav nun, 1941.

عدة صورة من البوم اولغا كاتان طالبة في مدرية Schmidt's Girls College في القدس . في الصورة الأولى تبين حصة في باحة المدرسة الداخلية برفقة صديقاتها بعمرؤ سبع سنوات ،اولغا كاتان هي الرابعة في الصف الأمامي اعتبارا من اليسار .تظهر في الصورة كذلك ألأم عرب والأب سونن ، مدير المدرسة. والى اليمن صورة اخذت سنة 1941، تبين حصة دراسية لراهية عربية وأخرى يوغسلافيه.

Left: The building that housed the Schmidt's Girls College boarding school. This photo was taken in the 1950s, when the school was under Israeli control. The school was moved to Nablus Street in front of the Damascus Gate.

Right: Students from Schmidt's Girls College during a visit to the Al-Aqsa Mosque, 1945.

عمارة فيها مدرسة Schmidt's Girls College الداخلية. الصورة تعود لسنة 1950، في تلك الفترة وقعت المدرسة في قبضة إسرائيل. وقد نقلت الى شارع نابلس قبالة بوابة دمشق.

طالبات المدرسة المذكورة خلال زيارتهم لمسجد الأقصى سنة 1945

A school trip to the Jordan River. A group of students surround Father Kerls and a teacher in charge of the boarding school; two nuns are in the background. The photograph was taken by Olga Kattan.

مجموعة في رحلة الى نهر الأردن. في الصورة التي التقطت من قبل اولغا كتان تظهر مجموعة من الطلاب، والآب كيرلس، ومعلمة مكلفة بالمدرسة الداخلية.

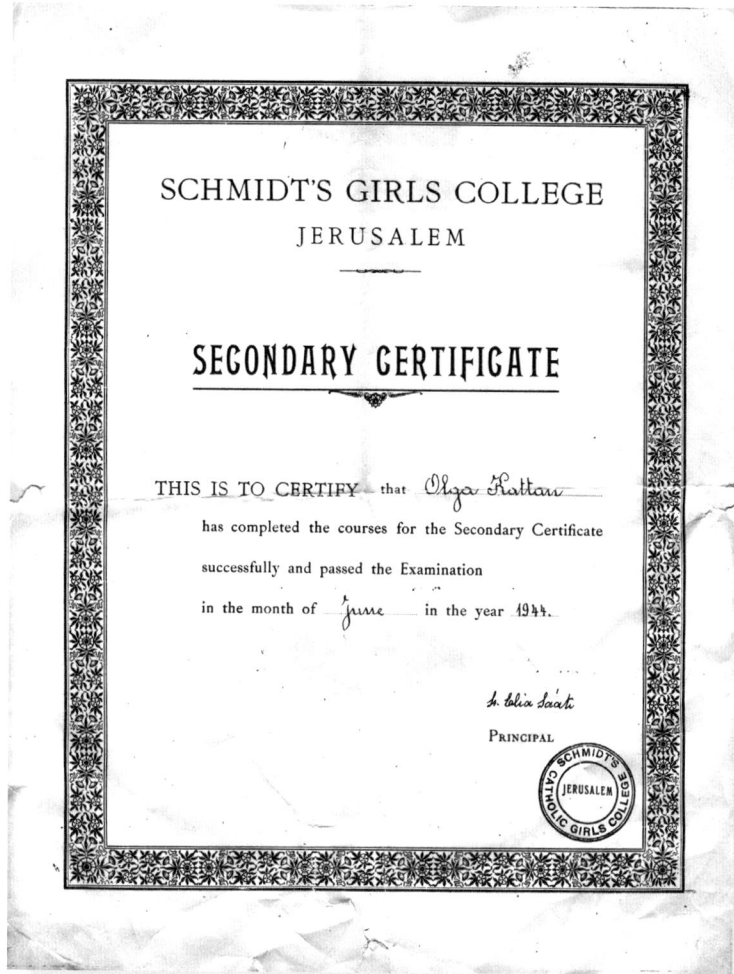

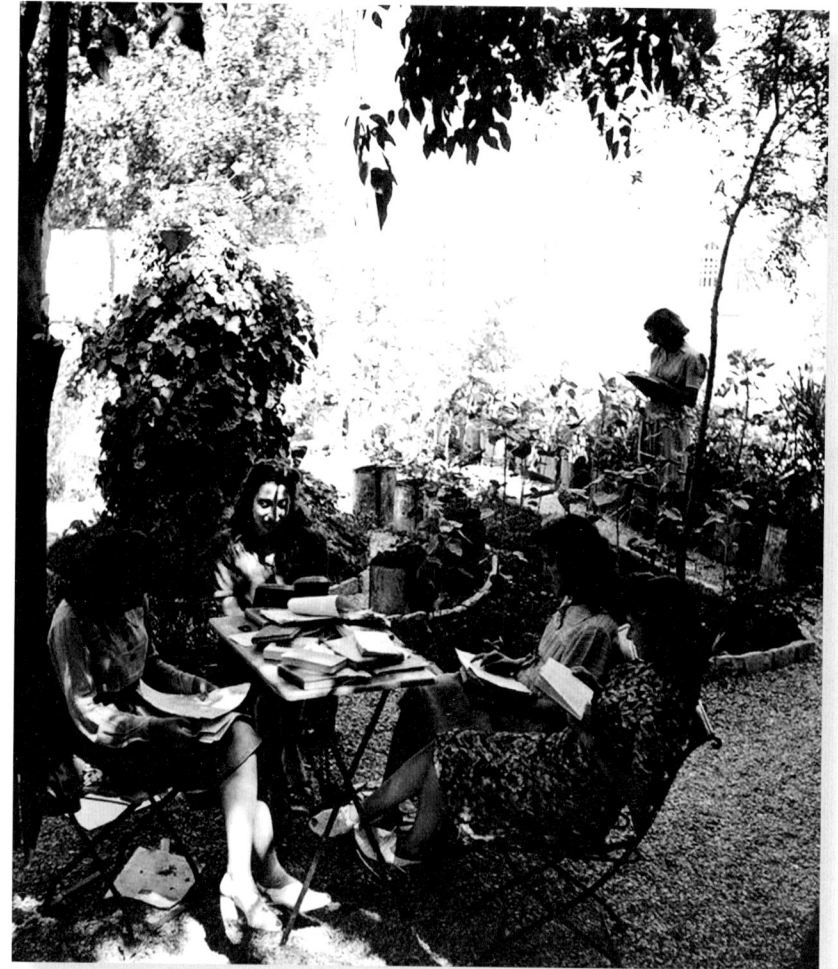

Left: A high school graduation certificate from Schmidt's Girls College, 1944.

Right: Young women studying in the school gardens, 1942.

شهادة مرحلة الثانوية سنة 1944.

الفتيات من مدرسة Schmidt's للفتيات في القدس، الى اليمين سنة 1942.

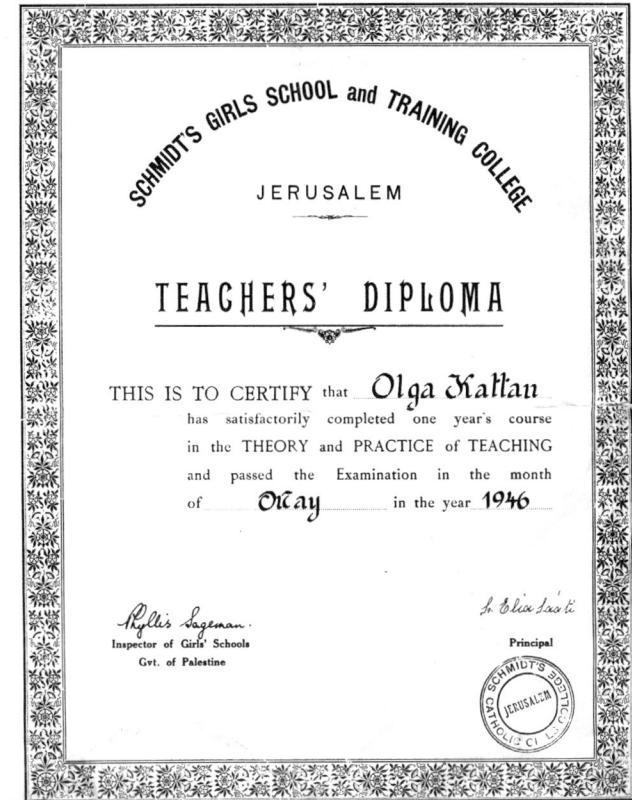

SCHMIDT'S GIRLS SCHOOL and TRAINING COLLEGE

JERUSALEM

TEACHERS' DIPLOMA

THIS IS TO CERTIFY that *Olga Kattan*
has satisfactorily completed one year's course
in the THEORY and PRACTICE of TEACHING
and passed the Examination in the month
of *May* in the year 1946

Phyllis Sageman
Inspector of Girls' Schools
Gvt. of Palestine

Principal

Left: A group of graduates with their teaching diplomas. Right: Olga Kattan's graduate teacher diploma.

مجموعة من الطلبة خريجو معهد التعليم، الى اليمين تظهر شهادة الدبلوم الذي تحصلت عليه أولغا كتان.

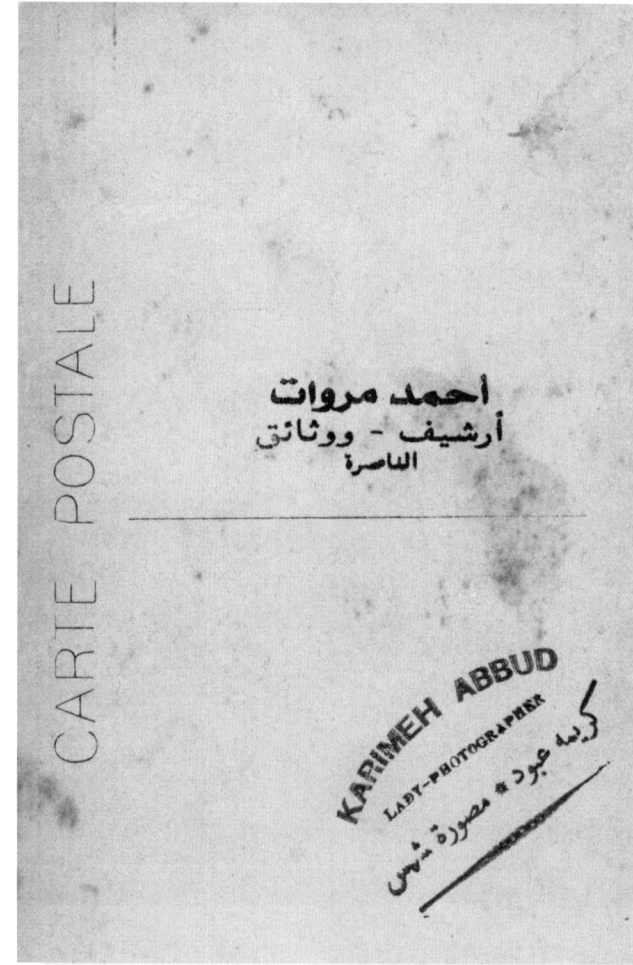

Left: Postcard featuring a photograph by Karima Abbud, titled "Two Girls from Nazareth," 1928. Karima Abbud was the first female Palestinian professional photographer, with studios in both Jerusalem and Haifa.

Right: The reverse side of the postcard with her stamp "Lady photographer."

كرت المعايدة بريدي صورة لكريمة عبود بعنوان فتاتان من الناصرة، اخذت سنة 1928. كريمة عبود هي أول مصورة محترفة فلسطينية تعمل في استوديو تصوير سواء في القدس أو حيفا.

خلفية كرت المعايدة يظهر ختمها (السيدة المصورة).

140

A child on a rooftop in Haifa. 1940s.

صورة طفل على سطح بيت في حيفا سنة 1940.

Left: Two friends on the beach in Haifa, April 20, 1942.

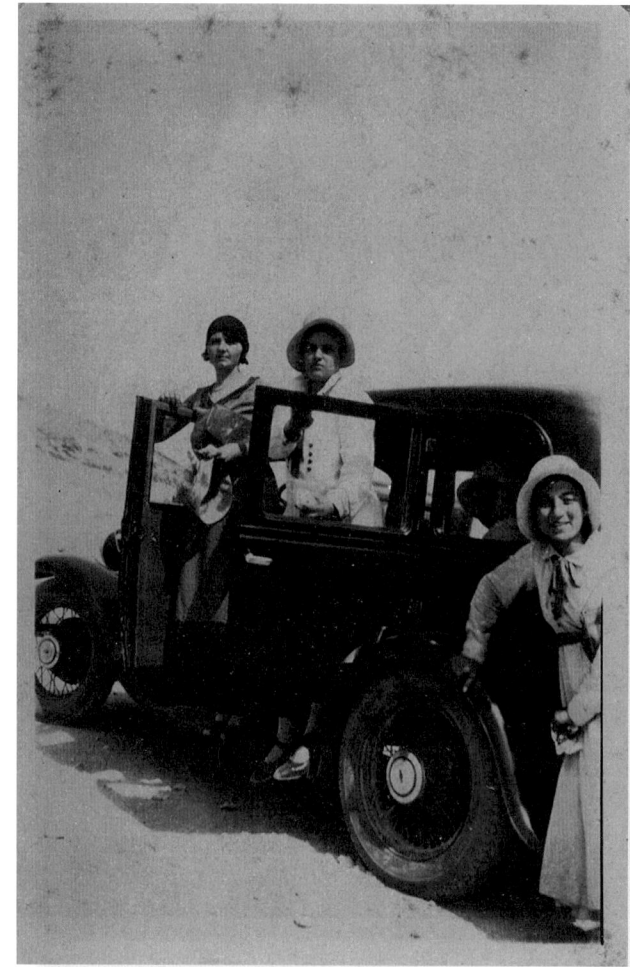

Right: Women posing in a car. From the Bahu family album (Haifa), 1942.

صديقان في شاطئ حيفا . تاريخ هذه الصورة 20 أبريل 1942. .الصورة الى اليمين : مجموعة من النساء يستعرضن في سيارة . صورة مأخوذة من الألبوم الخاص لعائلة باهوس من حيفا سنة 1942.

Left: Michel Saʿad playing the ʿoud.

Right: Saʿad with some friends in the old city of Haifa, March 23, 1934.

صورة ميشيل سعد يعزف على العود.

الصورة في اليمين: اخذت في 23 مارس سنة 1934، لسعد برفقة اصدقائه في الحي القديم لمدينة حيفا.

This page and the next: A group of friends on a picnic on Mount Carmel in Haifa, 1942.

في هذه الصفحة والصفحات التالية تجدون صورا لمجموعة من الأصدقاء خلال يوم العطلة ، أخذت في جبل الكرمل في حيفا سنة 1942.

Right: Friends at a restaurant in Haifa, 1942.

إلى اليمن : صورة لعدد الأصدقاء في أحد المطاعم بمدينة حيفا سنة 1942.

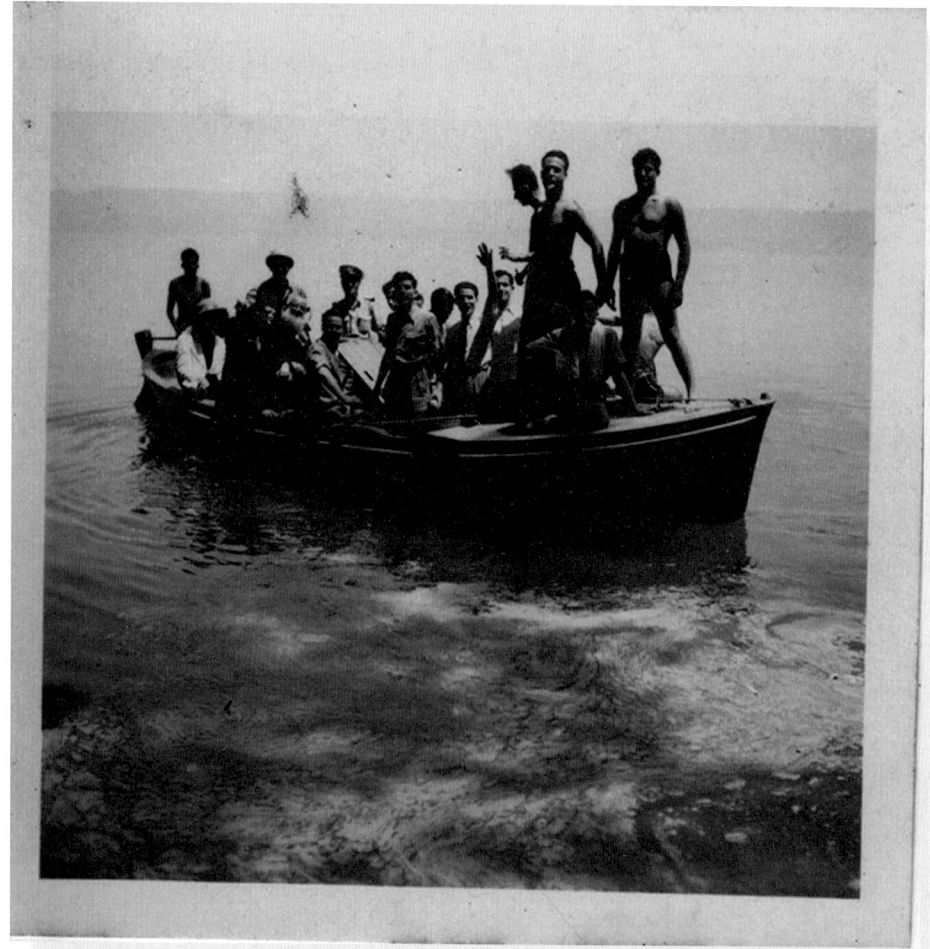

This page and the next: Friends on a day trip to Lake Tiberias, 1940–1942.

مجموعة صور لجمع من الأصدقاء ، اخذت خلال أحدى الرحلات في منطقة بحيرة طبريا خلال الفترة 1940- الى 1942.

Arab, Jewish, and British employees of the Haifa Customs Department, 1940.

صورتان لعمال (عرب ويهود وبريطانيون) يعملون في إدارة الجمارك بحيفا 1940.

Employees of the Haifa Customs Department. Shafika Sa'ad is in the center wearing a polka dot blouse. The two women on the left in the front row are Jewish. Photograph from Photo Sport Studio, Allenby Square, Haifa, 1940–1942.

صورة رائعة لموظفات في مصلحة الجمارك في حيفا : شفيقة سعد في وسط الصورة تلبس تنورة منقطة وفي الأسفل الى اليسار، يهوديات ، صورة استوديو (فوتو اسبورت) POB 64 Allemby Square, Haifa في حيفا 1940 – 1942.

Photographs from the Karameh family album. The Karamehs, from Haifa, are of Muslim Turkish origin. Left: Taher Karameh. Right: The Karameh family on the terrace of their home in Ibtin; Sami Karameh is in the center.

During the siege of Haifa in 1948, the family fled to their country home in Ibtin about ten miles east of Haifa. While they had planned to return in two weeks, they were never able to do so. Sami was the only family member who remained in Haifa.

صورة من الألبوم العائلي (عائلة كرامه) من حيفا، وهي عائلة مسلمة تركية الأصل.

سنة 1948 خلال حصار مدينة حيفا هربت العائلة الى مزعتها في إبطين التي تبعد 15 كم إلى الشرق من حيفا، وكانت تعتقد بأنها ستعود الى منزلها خلال اسبوعين. لم تعد هذه العائلة الى بيتها أبدا. سامي هو الشاب الوحيد الذي بقي، حيث قام باستخدام كمرته لتصوير عمليات هدم الحي القديم من قبل الإسرائيليين.

Left: A view of the Paris Square in the old city of Haifa, before it was demolished by Israeli troops. The photograph was taken by Sami Karameh from his car at the end of April 1948, when he went on a brief tour of the streets of his city after the capture of Haifa by the Haganah troops.

Right: Another image from the same day, showing what was once the center of the old city of Haifa, before it was demolished by Israeli troops. The old city had a bazaar similar to that of the Old City of Jerusalem.

الصورة الى اليسار التقطت من السيارة في مكان تم تدميره ، وهو ساحة باريس في مدينة حيفا القديمة ، تحول الآن الى مجرد تقاطع طرق.

والى اليمين نشاهد حيزا فارغا في وسط مدينة حيفا، قبل تدمير العمارات من قبل القوات الإسرائيلية خلال اجتياح مدينة حيفا، في هذا المكان بالذات كان يوجد بازار مماثل لتلك المنتشرة في القدس القديمة.

Haifa after the Israeli assault. Left: Two young people walking down a street in Haifa, the rubble from the Israeli assault on the city clearly visible.

اثنان من الشباب يتجولون في المنطقة المهدمة.

The old city of Haifa after the Israeli demolitions.

مشاهد أخرى لأثار الدمار الذي لحق بمدنية حيفا القديمة نتيجة اعمال الهدم المتعمدة التي قام بها الإسرائيليون.

Left: Girls pushing their belongings in strollers and wheelbarrows and fleeing Jaffa, 1948.

Right: A caravan of refugees and their belongings, fleeing from Gaza to Hebron in the West Bank, December 1949.

فتيات يجرون ممتلكاتهم بواسطة عربات هاربين من حيفا 1948.

قافلة من الجمال تنقل المهاجرين وأمتعتهم من غزة الخليل. ديسمبر 1948.

154

Palestinian refugees, initially displaced to the Gaza beach refugee camp, boarding boats to Lebanon and Egypt, 1949.

لاجئون فلسطينيون نقلوا في البداية الى مخيم في شاطئ غزة ، وانتقلوا فيما بعد الى لبنان ومصر سنة 1949 املا في العثور على ظروف افضل للحياة

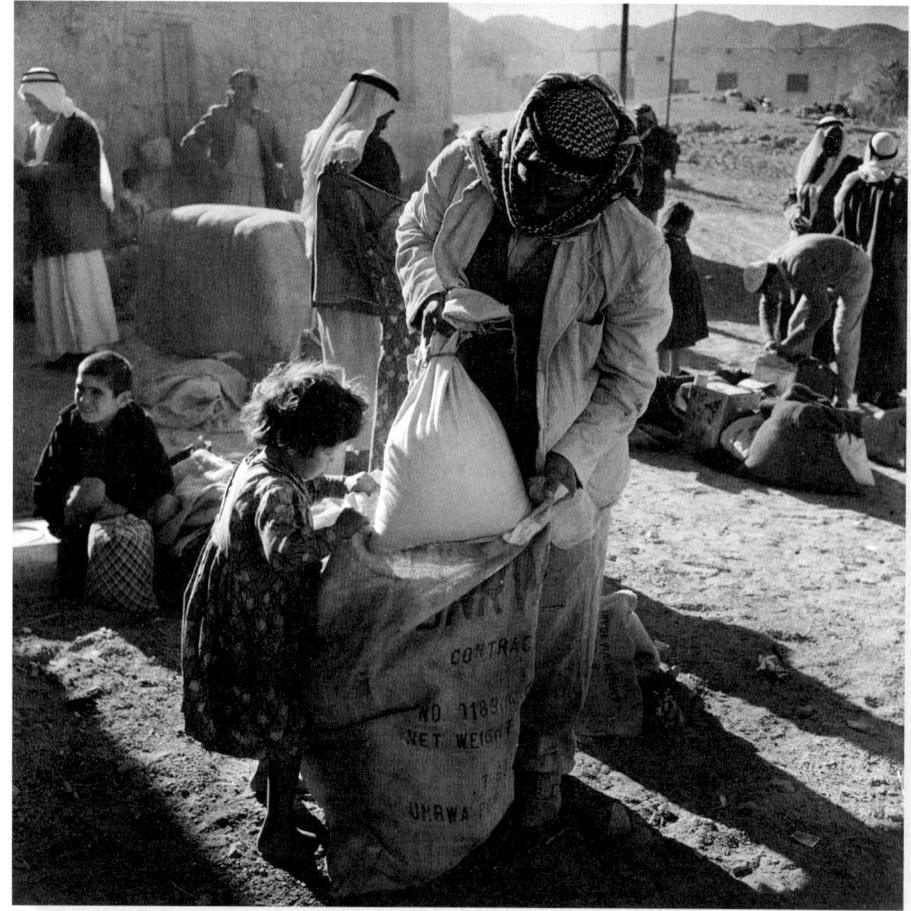

Left: The Nahr al-Bared refugee camp in Lebanon was one of the first to be set up as part of the emergency measures to shelter Palestinian refugees. Early 1950s.

Right: A man and his daughter collect their rations at a distribution point in Aqaba, Jordan. UNRWA trucks distributed rations every two months to refugees around Aqaba; there were no refugee camps in this town. Undated.

مخيم اللاجئين في النهر البارد (لبنان)هو اول المخيمات التي اقيمت بموجب الإجراءات العاجلة من اجل إيواء اللاجئين الفلسطينيين. السنوات الأولى من عقد الخمسينات.

رجل وابنته يتسلمون حصتهم من الأغذية في مركز التوزيع في العقبة (الأردن). شاحنات تابعة لوكالة غوث اللاجئين الأنروا قامت بتوزيع المخصصات الغذائية كل شهرين على اللاجئين في محيط العقبة ، حيث لم تتواجد مخيمات في هذه المنطقة (تاريخ غير محدد).

At first, the refugee camps were structured according to places of origin in Palestine, with the lives of its inhabitants revolving around the memory of their city, their village, their lost homes, and above all, around returning to Palestine. Later, nostalgia gave way to a strong sense of national identity. It is in the refugee camps where Palestinians, traumatized and torn apart by the Nakba, find the strength to rebuild, and where identity became a "Palestinian cause," that is, a national liberation movement.

نُظمت مخيمات اللاجئين الفلسطينيين في البداية، حسب المناطق التي قدموا منها في فلسطين، مما سمح بأن ترتبط حياة اللاجئين بشكل مباشر بالمناطق والقرى والمدن التي خرجوا منها، وتدور حول الذكريات التي تتعلق بالبيت والحارة والقرية مما جسد فكرة العودة الى فلسطين. وفيما بعد استبدلت مشاعر التشوق بمشاعر الانتماء والهوية الوطنية الفلسطينية، والمطالبة بالحقوق الوطنية. في مخيمات اللاجئين يجد المجتمع الفلسطيني المصدوم والممزق بسبب النكبة، القوة لاستعادة تجسيد الذات ، وفيها تكتسب الهوية الفلسطينية البعد اللازم لتصبح قضية فلسطينية، بعبارة أخرى حركة تحرير وه ي

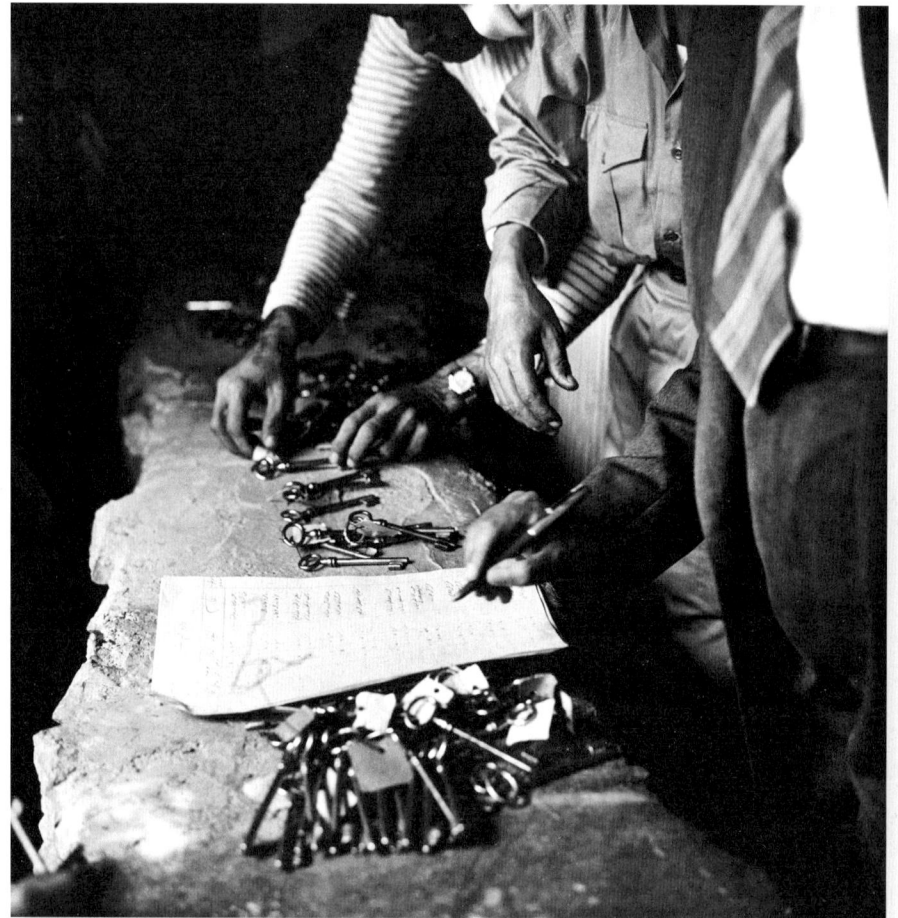

Left: Refugees in the Gaza Beach camp did not have running water in the 1950s. 1953.

Right: Keys to new concrete shelters in the Aida refugee camp, near Bethlehem. 1950.

في مخيم اللاجئين في شاطئ غزة لم تكن تتوفر المياه الجارية خلال الخمسينات. تاريخ هذه الصورة يعود الى1953.

مفاتيح ملاجئ من الإسمنت المسلح في مخيم عيدا بالقرب من بيت لحم. 1950.

One of the first preschool classes in the Dikwaneh refugee camp in Lebanon.

صورة من الحصص الأولى للتعليم في الروضة في مخيم ديكوانه بلبنان (بتاريخ غير محدد).

Girls playing basketball at the Center for Women's Activities in Kalandia, West Bank. 1950s.

مجموعة من الفتيات يمارسن لعبة كرة السلة في مركز النشاطات النسائية في قلنديا (الضفة الغربية) خلال عقد الخمسينيات.

Photo Credits

The G. Eric and Edith Matson Photograph Collection
The American Colony, 1881-1934. US Library of Congress. Pages 27–99*
*With the exception of two photographs on page 81

Mansour Collection
Pages 81/100–34*/140–53
*With the exception of two photographs on page 128 and the photo on the right on page 130
The photos in the Mansour collection were donated by the following families:
Medawar. al-Farra, Karameh. Abu Snina. Abyad. Saqqa. Bahos. Shayoun. Ihssan. Badran. Mattar

Nimer Yazbek Collection, of Nazareth
Page 128, two photos

Olga Kattan—Cantarabia Archive
Page 130, photo on the right. Pages 135–39

UNRWA
Pages 154–60

On This Earth

We have on this earth what makes life worth living: April's hesitation, the
  aroma of bread
at dawn, a woman's point of view about men, the works of Aeschylus, the
  beginning
of love, grass on a stone, mothers living on a flute's sigh and the invaders' fear
  of memories.

We have on this earth what makes life worth living: the final days of
  September, a woman
keeping her apricots ripe after forty, the hour of sunlight in prison, a cloud
  reflecting a swarm
of creatures, the peoples' applause for those who face death with a smile,
  a tyrant's fear of songs.

We have on this earth what makes life worth living: on this earth, the Lady
  of Earth,
mother of all beginnings and ends. She was called Palestine. Her name
  later became
Palestine. My Lady, because you are my Lady, I deserve life.

Mahmoud Darwish, Palestinian poet born in Al Birwa, Galilee, 1941-2008. From Mahmoud Darwish, *Unfortunately, It Was Paradise: Selected Poems*, translated by Amira El-Zein, Carolyn Forché, Munir Akash, Sinan Antoon (Berkeley, University of California Press, 2013), 6.

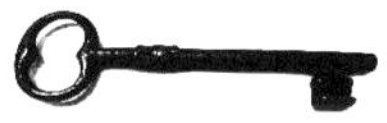

عَلَى هَذِهِ الأَرْض

عَلَى هَذِهِ الأَرْضِ مَا يَسْتَحِقُّ الحَيَاةَ: تَرَدُّدُ إبريلَ, رَائِحَةُ الخُبْزِ في
الفَجْرِ, آراءُ امرأةٍ في الرِّجالِ, كِتَابَاتُ أَسْخِيْلِيوس، أوّلُ الحُبِّ، عشبٌ
عَلَى حَجَرٍ، أُمَّهاتٌ تَقِفْنَ عَلَى خَيْطِ نايٍ, وخوفُ الغُزَاةِ مِنَ الذِّكْرِيَاتِ.

عَلَى هَذِهِ الأَرْضِ ما يَسْتَحِقُّ الحَيَاةَ: نِهَايَةُ أيلُولَ، سَيِّدَةٌ تترُكُ
الأَرْبَعِينَ بِكَامِلِ مشمِشِهَا, ساعَةُ الشَّمْسِ في السِّجْنِ، غَيْمٌ يُقَلِّدُ سِرْباً مِنَ
الكَائِنَاتِ، هُتَافَاتُ شَعْبٍ لِمَنْ يَصْعَدُونَ إلى حَتْفِهِم بَاسِمِينَ, وَخَوْفُ
الطُّغَاةِ مِنَ الأُغْنِيَاتِ.

عَلَى هَذِهِ الأَرْضِ مَا يَسْتَحِقُّ الحَيَاةَ: عَلَى هَذِهِ الأَرْضِ سَيِّدَةُ
الأَرْضِ، أُمُّ البِدَايَاتِ، أُمُّ النِّهَايَاتِ. كَانَتْ تُسَمَّى فِلسْطِين. صَارَتْ تُسَمَّى
فلسْطِين. سَيِّدَتِي: أَستحِقُّ، لأنَّكِ سَيِّدَتِي، أَسْتَحِقُّ الحَيَاةَ.

محمود درويش

محمود درويش. شاعر فلسطيني ولد في البروة، في الجليل (1941-2008).

رمل زيتا	المنشية	الشوك التحتا	المالكية
طابور	المنصورة	الشنة	ملاحة
ام خالد	نصر الدين	طيطبة	المنشية
وادي الحوارث	نمرين	تليل	المنصورة
وادي قباني	النقيب	العلمانية	منصورة الخايط
خربة الزبادة	سمخ السمكية	العريفية	ماروش
خربة زلفة .	السمرا	الويزرية	ميرون
	الشجرة	يردا	المفتخرة
	الطابغة	الزنجرية	مخر الخايط
	العبيدية	الزاوية	خربة المنطار
	خربة الوعرة السوداء	السوق الفوقاني	النبي يوشع
	يعقوق	السوق التحتاني .	النعيمة
	وادي الحمام .		قبعة

قضاء طولكرم

قضاء طبرية

		عولم	قداس
خربة بيت ليد		الدلهمية	قديته
بيارات حانون		ابو شوشة	القيطية
فردوسيا		حدثا	القديرية
غابات كفر السور		الحمة	الرأس الاحمر
الجلمة		حطين	سبلان
كفر سابا		كفر سبت	سفسر
قاقون		لوبيا	صالحة
المجدل		معذر	الصالحية
خربة المنشية		المجدل	الساموي
مسكة		المنارة	الصنبرية
			سعسع

165

الظاهرية التحتا	التينه	جيمزو	أبو شوشة
الدربشية	الطيره	خروبة	عجنجول
الدرارة	أم كلخة	الخيمة	عاقير
الفارا	وادي حنين	خلدة	برفيلية
الفرادية	يبني	الكنيسة	البرية
فرعيم	خربة زكريا	اللطرون	بشيت
الغباطية	زرنوقة .	المغر	بيت فار
غرابة		مجدل يابا	بيت جيز
الحمرا	**قضاء صفد**	المنصورة	بيت نبالة
الحراوي		المخيزم	بيت شنة
حنين	العباسية	المزيرعة	بيت سوسين
الحسينية	القمح	النعاني	بيت معين
جاهولة	أكبره	النبي روبين	بير سليم
الجوانه	علمة	قطرة	البرج
جوب يوسف	عموقة	قزازه	خربة البوايرة
كفر برعيم	عرب الشمالين	القباب	دانيال
الخالصة	عرب الزبيد	القبيبة	دير ابو سلامة
خان الدوير	عين الزيتون	قولا	دير أيوب
خربة كرازة	بيسمون	سجد	دير محاسين
الخساس	البرية	سلبيت	دير طريف
خيام الوليد	البطيحة	صرفند العمار	خربة الظاهرية
كراد البقارة	البويزية	صرفند الخراب	الحديثة
كراد الغنامة	دلاتا	صيدون	إدنه
لزازة	الدوارة	شهمة	عنابة
مداحيل	ديشوم	شلطة	جليا

قصلة
نطاف
القابو
راس ابو عمار
صرعة
سفلى
خربة العمر .

قضاء جنين

عين المنسي
خربة الجوفه
اللجون
المزار
نورس
زرعين .

قضاء الناصرة

صفورية
أندور
المجيدل
معلول .

قضاء الرملة

أبو الفضل

خربة اللوز	الحرم	**قضاء الخليل**	الطنطورة	إم الزينات
خربة الشيخ	إجليل	أم البرج	الطيرة	إم الشوف
دير ياسين	إجليل الشمالية	بركوسيا	عرب ظهرة الضميري	برة قيسارية
قالونيا	الجماسين الغربي	بيت جبرين	عرب الفقراء	بريكة
الولجة	الجماسين الشرقي	بيت نتيف	عرب نفيعات	البطيمات
المالحة	جريشة	تل الصافي	عين غزال	بلد الشيخ
عين كارم	الخيرية	الدوايمة	عين حوض	جبع
دير رافات	رنتية	دير الدبان	الغبية التحتا	الجلمة
دير الهوى	السافرية	دير النخاس	الغبية الفوقا	خبيزة
ساريس	ساقية	رعنا	قنير	خربة البرج
بيت نقوبا	سلمة	زكريا	قيرة	خربة الدامون
علار	السوالمة	ذكرين	قيسارية	خربة السرسك
عقور	الشيخ مؤنس	زيتا	كبارة	سعسع
عرطوف	كفر عانة	عجور	كفر لام	خربة الشونة
بيت عتاب	المر	القبيبة	الكفرين	خربة القصاير
بيت ثول	المسعودية	كدنة	المزار	قمبازة
بيت ام الميس	المويلح	مغلس .	المنسي	خربة لد
البراية	يازور .		النغنغية	خربة المنارة
دير إيبان		**قضاء يافا**	هوشة	خربة المنصورة
دير عمر	**قضاء القدس**	العباسية	وداي عارة	دالية الروحاء
اشوا	سطاف	ابو كشك	وعرة السريس	الريحانية
عصلين	القسطل	بيت دجن	ياجور	السنديانة
خربة اسم الله	صوبا	بيار عدس	عتليت .	خربة السوامير
خربة جرش	بيت محسير	فجة		صبارين
الجورة	لفتة			صرفند

ال418 قرية مدمرة في فلسطين

				قضاء عكا
السوافير الغربية	برير	الطيره	المنشية	إقرت
صميل	البطاني الشرقي	عرب البواطي	المنصوره	إم الفرج
عراق سويدان	البطاني الغربي	عرب الصفا	ميعار	البروة
عراق المنشية	بعلين	عرب العريضة	النبي روبين	البصة
عرب صقرير	بيت جرجة	الغزاوية	النهر	تربيخا
الفالوجة	بيت دراس	الفاتور		التل
قسطينة	بيت طيما	فرونة	**قضاء بيسان**	خربة جدين
كرتيا	بيت عفا	قومية	الأشرفية	خربة عربي
كوفخة	تل الترمس	كفرة	ام عجره	الدامون
كوكبا	جسير	كوكب الهوا	البيره	دير القاسي
المحرقة	الجلدية	المرصص	تل الشوك	الرويس
المسمية الصغيرة	الجورة	مسيل الجزل	جبول	الزيب
المسمية الكبيرة	جولس	يُبلى .	الحمرا	سمحاتا
نجد	الجية		الحميدية	سروح
نعليا	حتا	**قضاء بئر السبع**	خربة ام صابونة	السميرية
هربيا	حليقات	الجمامة	خربة الزاوية	عرب السمنية
هوج	حمامة	الخلصة	خربة الطاقة	عمقا
ياصور .	الخصاص	العمارة .	الخُنيزير	الغبيسية
	دمرة		دنة	الكابري
قضاء حيفا	دير سنيد	**قضاء غزة**	زبعة	كفر عنان
أبو زريق	سمسم	إسدود	الساخنة	كويكات
ابو شوشة	السوافير الشرقية	بربره	السامرية	
إجزم	السوافير الشمالية	برق	سرين	

168

في الصور التي تم تحويلها الى رقمية من المسودّة، أو الشرائح الزجاجية مباشرةً، تعمدنا الإبقاء على إطارِ الفيلم الأسود حولها، وعلى ترقيمها، الذي يبدو لنا، أحياناً، بقايا شريط لاصق، كما أبقينا على الملاحظات المدونة، فكلُّ ذلك، بعيداً عن نقطة ضعفي كمصورة، يعطيها قيمة وثائقية. إن الملاحظات المدونة على هذه الصور والتي تظهر معلومات زمانيةٍ ومكانيةٍ حول موقع التصوير مهمّة على وجه الخصوص. الملاحظات تظهر معكوسةً, لكنها إذا ما شوهدت بواسطة مرآة، وهي لعبة أقترحها على المشاهد، ستُظهِّرها (لن يكون هناك تعبير أفضل)، هذا ما يحدث أساساً مع الصور العائدة إلى مجموعة ماتسون.

من هذه المجموعة استنسخنا عدة صور ثلاثية الأبعاد كنوع من الفضول والتوثيق، ولكننا استغنينا في الغالب عن نصف الصورة.

رغبةً منّا في المحافظة على الطابع الشخصيّ والأجواء العائلية الحميمة لهذه الألبومات قرّرنا استنساخَ الحوامل التي تؤطّر الصور، والأوراق المقوّاة التي كانت تشكل صفحات هذه الألبومات التي لصقت عليها الصور، بما في ذلك ما ورد مدّوناً فيها من ملاحظات. إنّها الأوراق المقوّاة والصور المجعّدة والمطويةالتي توحي بالتلف. الدافع ذاته هو الذي جعلنا نُقرّر ألا نمسّ التجاعيد، وخاصّة الطيات وآثار الأيدي التي قلّبت الصفحات وهي ترتاح فوق الذكريات؛ قرّرنا أن نحترم عدة آثار أجيال مرتاحة فوق هذه الصور.

ساندرا باريلارو

مصورة

في حيفا استطعنا أن ننعم بكرم ضيافة فلسطيني الثانية والأربعين، الذين لم يتمكّن "الإسرائيليون من نفيهم لأسبابٍ مختلفة، وهم في الواقع مجموعة بشرية حيوية، متماسكة ومقاومة. لقد أتيحت لنا فرصة حضور العديد من النشاطات الثقافية الفلسطينية، ومظاهرة انطلقت تضامناً مع السجناء الفلسطينيين. شعرنا بالغضب والأسى الشديد عندما رأينا كيف تُركت عكا، تلك المدينة القديمة تهدّم. كما تأكّدنا بأمّ أعيننا من التدمير المتواصل والتدريجي والمتعمّد أيضاً لمدينة حيفا القديمة، المدينة العربية الموجودة قبل قيام إسرائيل سنة 1948 بكثير. شاهدنا من على هضبة منزلَ عائلة غسان كنفاني الجميل الذي يطلّ على البحر، خاوياً ومهجوراً بعد أن طُرِدَ قاطنوه، وهم اليوم لاجئون مثلهم مثل الكثيرين من المنحدرين منهم.

وبالعودة إلى موضوع الصور، فإنّ هذه الرحلة وإمكانية العثور على البوماتِ صورٍ أخرى بيّنت لنا أن غالبية الصور تنتي لعائلات برجوازية حضرية حيفاوية. لسنا بصدد "إجراء إحصائية" لصور المجتمع الفلسطيني وقتذاك، فهذه الصور لوحدها كانت كفيلة بإظهار مشهدٍ جزئي ومختزل بل ومشوهٍ أيضاً. كان علينا أن نضع هذه المجموعة من الصور الشخصية في إطار أشملَ من الصور، التي تُقرّبنا من فلسطين تلك السنين، التي كانت تجري فيها الاستعدادات لطرد وتشتيت سكانها.

وبتقفينا لأثر بعض الصور عثرنا على كنزٍ آخر: أرشيف صور فندق امريكان كولوني في القدس، المعروفة بمجموعة ماتسون، إنّها مجموعة هائلة من مسودات تصل إلى ما يزيد عن 22 ألف مسودّة ولوح زجاجيّ. الكثير منها صور بانورامية لفلسطين. هذه المجموعة موجودة في مكتبة الكونجرس الأمريكي، حُوّل معظمها إلى صور رقمية، وهي متاحة لكلّ من يريد أن يشاهدها بحرية من خلال بوابته على الشبكة العنكبوتية.

التُقطت صور هذه المجموعة ما بين 1898 و 1946، وتشتمل على صور على علاقة بالعادات والمشاهير والأحداث الاجتماعية والسياسية، كتلك التي التُقطَت خلال الاحتجاجات المتكررة ضد ما كان يُحَسّ بأنّه غزو صهيوني، والأعياد الشعبية، والمصانع، والمهن. الخ . صور عالية الجودة والجمال، حلم لي كمصورة، واكتشاف ملأنا بالحماس لأنه كان سيسمح لنا بإكمال الدائرة.

إيضاحات فنية مختصرة

في الكثير من الحالات، إن لم يكن من المستحيل، تحديدُ تاريخ مُعَيّن للصور التي ننشرها في هذا الكتاب. الصور التي تنتي إلى مجموعة ماتسون تحتفظ بالتاريخ الدقيق لالتقاطها أو نشرها، في بعض الحالات، وفي حالات أخرى تُغطّي هذه المعلومات فترةً طويلة جدّاً تجعلها غير دقيقة. ومع ذلك قرّرنا الإبقاء عليها لعدم وجود معلومات دقيقة. قليلة جدّاً الصور التي نستطيع أن نعطي تاريخاً دقيقاً لالتقاطها، عندما تظهر هذه ويكون على ظهرها كتابة بقلم رصاص هذا يعني لنا فرحة عظيمة وارتياحاً. نعتقد أن من المهمّ أن نُحَدِّدَ قدر المستطاع الفضاء الزمني وأن نربط هذه الصور التلقائية، الشخصيّة والحميمة بالأحداث التي كانت ترسم أفقَ مستقبل فلسطين، والكارثة التي كانت تتربص بشعبها.

كل صورة هي شهادة على الوجود (رولاند بارتر) الكاميرا الذكية

ما دام هناك احتلال وبقي هناك لاجئون علينا أن نواصل التذكير، فالذكريات لا يمكن أن تُغزى أو تُجتث.نعلم قوّة الاستحضار أو بحسب بصيرة الشاعر: نعرف جيداً مدى خوف الغزاة *من الذكريات*.

على الرغم من معرفتنا بمنشورات من الصور سابقة رائعة وخلاقة تعود لفترة ما قبل 1948، كـكتاب وليد الخالدي: *قبل شتاته*، أو العمل الذي أخرجه لنا إلياس صنبر *الفلسطينيون* الذي يجمع بين دفتيه صوراً منذ 1839 وحتى يومنا، فقد قررنا الصحفية تِرسا أرانغورن وأنا شخصياً المساهمة بما نستطيع لدعم *الذاكرة الحيّة* للشعب، للمجتمع الفلسطيني، لفلسطين التي كانت موجودة قبل النكبة بكثير. علينا مواصلة التذكير، وتسليط الضوء من جديد على مشاهد كانت قد رسمت يوماً ما بالنور، ونشر صور الـتُقطت للنطاق العائلي وإطار الصداقة، ليتم تداولها حول فنجان قهوة في زمن كان المجتمع ينسج نفسه بخيوط مختلفة تماماً. صور التقطت في عهد لم يكن الابتذال بالصورة منتشراً إلى هذا الحد.

صورٌ أمدّها الزمنُ وكارثةُ الشعب الفلسطيني ببعدٍ ومعنى آخرين. صور تلقائيّة كتاكتيّة تقدّمنا في اكتشافها كلّما امتلأنا عجباً ودهشة، رقة وغضباً ... لأجل عالم ضائع، لأجل أناس طُردوا من حياتهم ومن عالمهم وأرضهم. مجتمع هزّته صدمةُ الطرد، ولم يعد هو ذاته. صورٌ تُظهر لنا براءة حركاتٍ يومية، غريبة تماماً عمّا كان سيحيق بها دون حتى أن يخطر بالبال أنها ستكون الأخيرة بمعان كثيرة.

صورٌ مجتمعة تتطلّع إلى أن تُذكّر بالظرف الإنساني لمجتمع لن يكون بالإمكان محوه ولا اجتثاثه. صور شخصية تُقرّبنا من ذواتنا، من عائلاتنا ومن أسلافنا ، تذكّرنا بألبوماتنا العائلية ذاتها.

بدأنا البحث عن صور غير منشورة من قبل بهدف إثراء هذه الذاكرة. المهمة التي لم تكن سهلة نظراً لأنّ الصورة في النصف الأول من القرن العشرين لم تكن شيئاً شعبياً، بمعنى أن تملك كلُّ عائلةٍ آلةَ تصوير أو تعدّ ألبوماً عائلياً. كانت الصورة ترفاً، لا يطاله في غالبيته زراعي كالمجتمع الفلسطيني في تلك الفترة. أضيف إلى ذلك أنه حدث، بعد 1948، شتات ونفي وتشتتٌ بشرٍ وممتلكات، من بينها الصور.

من حسن الحظّ أنّنا وقعنا خلال عملية البحث، على البروفيسور جوني منصور من مدينة حيفا، وهو دارس مُتَيّم بمدينته وتاريخها، راح كأريادنا يشدّ "خيطَ *الذاكرة* [2] التصويرية، حتى شكّل مجموعة من الصور العائلية. راح منصور يرفع الحجاب ويكشف لنا شيئاً فشيئاً عن هذه الصور،. التي بحث عنها من بيت إلى بيت، من عائلة إلى عائلة، ومن البوم إلى آخر، وراحت تصلنا هذه الجواهر الفوتوغرافية الصغيرة بالبريد الالكتروني. قررنا أنا وترِسا السفر إلى حيفا بحثاً عن بقيّة الكنز.

لكن قبل موعدنا مع منصور في يافا، قرّرنا قضاء عدة أيام في البحث عن البومات صور لعائلات أخرى، وقمنا بزيارة بعض الأصدقاء في رام الله، وبيت لحم، والقدس... في الأسابيع السابقة على عملية هامش الحماية على غزّة، راح الجيش الإسرائيلي معززاً بالمستوطنين "يمشّط" الضفة الغربية ويزرع الرعب فيها، بحثاً عن ثلاثة من المستوطنين المراهقين في محيط الخليل. ومرّة أخرى كانت الضفة الغربية "مقلوبة رأساً على عقب"، نقاط تفتيش مُشدّدة، مستوطنون يقطعون الطرق، غارات في كلّ مكان؛ ومرّة أخرى كان القتلى يقطرون من الجانب الفلسطيني. حَدَسْنا من خلال الدماثة الإسرائيلية غير المعهودة في مطار تل أبيب بأنّ شيئاً ما يُبيّت...

وبالرغم من أنَّ الصورة الفوتوغرافية هي جامدة بكونها هكذا، إلا أن ما فيها يتحرك على محور الزمن والمكان بفعل الذاكرة الجمعية والفردية التي تعرف كيفية التعامل مع الصورة.

أنني أتعامل مع مواد تاريخية متنوعة: النصوص(الوثائق والأوراق الشخصية والعامة)، الصور الفوتوغرافية، والتاريخ الشفوي المتعلق بفلسطين، ولكن بوجه خاص مدينتي حيفا التي ولدت فيها وأعيش فيها.

بدأت اتعامل مع تاريخ هذه المدينة التي تمّ ترحيل سكانها الفلسطينيين في 1948 بصورة وبطريقة بشعة جدًّا، بحيث لم يبق من 75 ألف فلسطيني سوى ثلاثة آلاف فقط. والأكثر بشاعة من هذا، أن المؤسسة الرسمية الإسرائيلية من حكومة وبلدية تنكر أنها كانت السبب في التهجير، وترفض الاعتراف بأنها تتحمل مسؤولية النكبة لهذه المدينة ولباقي أجزاء فلسطين. ومع مرور الزمن ونتيجة لتراكم كبير للصور والوثائق بدأت بنشرها بطريقة تنظيم معارض لصور المدينة التي جمعتها من البومات العائلات ومن الأرشيفات وغيرها من المصادر. وفي كل معرض ألاحظ حركة المشاهدين والمهتمين والعابرين. إنّ سلوك الناظرين إلى الصور وتعابيرهم الخارجية ثم تعبيرهم الكلامي(اللفظي) يعكس نوعا من التفاعل مع الصورة وبالتالي مع الموضوع الذي تحمله الصور مجتمعة.

النص + الصورة يعززان معاً الرواية التاريخية للشعب الفلسطيني.

هذه الميكانيكية المبسطة في مظهرها الخارجي تعكس لنا مشهدية رائعة وجميلة لمجتمع ديناميكي عمل على بناء ذاته الفكرية والاجتماعية والاقتصادية والثقافية والتعليمية وغيرها لينتقل بالتالي من مجتمع ريفي إلى مجتمع مدني متقدم. إن الصور بالذات بمعظمها قد تمّ التقاطها بالمدن التي توفرت فيها استديوهات ومصورين ميدانيين وامتلكت عائلات كثيرة آلات تصوير خاصة بها... أكثر من القرى في الريف... كلّها، أي الصور التي اجتمعت لدي ساعدتني في فهم هذه الديناميكية.

اعتقد بكل قوة أن الشعب الفلسطيني الذي فقد أرضه رغما عنه ولأسباب أتينا على بعضها سابقا، يحاول ألا يفقد تاريخه. ولأني من ابناء هذا الشعب الذي أعيش يومياً مآسيه أعرف مدى صدق علاقته بأرضه ووطنه وماضيه وتاريخه وصوره ووثائقه... لأنها كلها مجتمعة تعيد إليه ما هو بحاجة إليه. وحاجته إلى الوطن.

بقلم د. جوني منصور – محاضر ومؤرخ فلسطيني مقيم في مدينة حيفا.

172

فالتاريخ الشفوي بهذا السياق هو أداة للتعريف بالمكان، والعودة إليه من خلال الذات الفلسطينية الصرفة، وعيشه بالحقائق والكلمات والأحاسيس وصور الماضي التي لم تفارق الفلسطيني أبدا، بل بالعكس ما زالت تتفاعل بقوة وعمق في تشكيل ذاكرته التاريخية الفردية والجمعية. وما يُعزّز هذا التاريخ ما بقي في ذاكرة الفلسطينيين من تفاصيل ومعلومات حياتية وشخصية وعامة عن مجرى حياتهم اليومي. ويتعزز هذا الجانب بما لديهم من صور فوتوغرافية ووثائق حافظوا عليها وبقيت في حوزتهم بالرغم من تنقلهم وترحالهم من مكان لآخر.

إذن، هناك علاقة قوية بين الزمان والمكان والصورة الفوتوغرافية التي باعتقادي أقوى شاهد على ما جرى وعلى مشهدية الحياة.

صحيح ان الصورة أمر جامد حصل في لحظة زمنية محددة، ولا يمكن استرجاعها فيزيا، اي عمليا. إلا أن هذا الجمود هو في حد ذاته ما يميزها بكونها تنقل لنا معلومات وتفاصيل مرّت عبر الزمن، وهي – اي الصورة – تتيح امامي أنا الناظر فرصة كبيرة بالعودة عبر نفق الزمان إلى زمن الصورة وإلى المكان الذي تم فيه التقاطها.

كما نلاحظ أنّ حيّز الذاكرة الشفوية والتاريخ الشفوي يحمل غاية مركزية وهي تأصيل الوجود الفلسطيني في المكان الفلسطيني بالرغم من أنه ـ أي الفلسطيني ـ قد طُرد منه عنوة وبالقوة وبوحشية كبيرة. ومن جهة أخرى يريد الفلسطيني استعادة الزمان الذي انتهى بواسطة رسم صورة جذابة ورائعة وأحياناً كثيرة بريئة لقريته ومدينته، وكأنها الجنة في ذاتها. ووسط عملية الاستعادة هذه يطفو على السطح الواقع الحقيقي.

لهذا، أعتقد أنه يجب ألّا تبقى الذاكرة الشفوية الفلسطينية محصورة أو محجوزة في إطار "أيّام زمان"، بل وبالإمكان توجيهها واستخراجها بما يضمن تصور زمني مستقبلي فيه الأمل القوي بإمكانية العودة إلى المكان، وهذه العودة ممكنة. مفهوم العودة الفلسطينية المطبق حالياً هو عملية إسترجاعية تاريخية تحضيراً للمستقبل، فالماضي الذي نتعامل معه كماضٍ ليس هكذا إلا بما له من مخزون يدعم الحق.

وعلاقة الزمان بالمكان وبالعكس هي صورة ليس بالضرورة تحقيقها كما هي، إذ لا يمكن فكريا تحقيق العودة إلى زمن، ما يمكن تحقيقه هو العودة إلى المكان بزماننا معتمدين على التاريخ الشفوي الفلسطيني مثلا كجزء من بناء متجدد للعلاقة ما بين الفلسطيني والمكان.

المكان تغير، الزمان لدى الفلسطينيين في اللجوء والشتات قد توقف عند لحظة التهجير حاملا معه صورة المدينة والقرية في حينه، إلا أن صورة المكان هذه لم تعد كما هي، فالاستعادة خيالية أو نوستالجية تدفع بالتالي إلى الحفاظ على الموروث المكاني غير الملموس في غالب الأحيان. وهذا اللاملموس هو قائم في الصورة الفوتوغرافية التي تحمل إشارات بصرية لها معان مفهومة لدى الناظر إليها، ولكنها في واقع الأمر قد تغيرت تفاصيل المكان الذي التقطت فيها، كما أشرت سابقا.

إذن، هذه الجدلية بين الزمان والمكان ستبقى تلاحق وترافق الفلسطيني أينا ذهب وأينما حلَّ لأنّها جزء نفسيّ وفكريّ من تكوينه الإنساني.

إن الصورة الفوتوغرافية التي تنسجم في الزمان والمكان لها ثلاثة دلالات: الايقونة والدليل والرمز. فبالنسبة لكونها ايقونة فإنها واقع معين حصل أثناء عملية التصوير، لا يمكن إعادته. في حين انها تؤشر إلى من فيها من اشخاص ومعالم. أما ما ترمز إليه فهو امر يفهمه (وقد لا يفهمه) المتصفح للصورة.

فالصورة عبارة عن رسالة تحمل في محتوياتها الظاهرة والخفية التي يراها بطريقته الخاصة الباحث والمتصفح لها. رسالة الصورة الفوتوغرافية عبارة عن عملية عودة إلى الوراء بواسطة الذاكرة. الذاكرة ليست بالضرورة للذين يعرفون من يظهر أو ما يظهر في الصورة، إنما ما يحمله من معرفة تتعزز بالصورة.

الصورة الفوتوغرافية نصٌّ تاريخي يُعزِّز البقاء

منذ أن تفتحت عيناي وفلسطين حاضرة في كل تفاصيل حياتي. فأولاً من البيت حيث أن والدي مُهجرين قد تعرّضا إلى كل عمليات التهجير التي أصابت الشعب الفلسطيني في العام 1948. ثم من خلال خبرتي وعيشي في أحد أحياء حيفا الفقيرة والمهملة "حي وادي النسناس"، ومن المدرسة الثانوية التي زوّدتني بمعرفة هامة لصقل هويتي الوطنية. ومن خلال متابعاتي لما كان يجري من حولنا محليًا وقطريًا وإقليميًا. وهكذا نَمَتْ وكبرتْ القضيةُ الفلسطينية مع نموي الجسدي والفكري والتوعوي. حضور فلسطين ليس فقط من باب الذكريات التي نقلها إليّ والدي أو أعمامي وأفراد آخرين من العائلة، إنما ما قمت به بواسطة هذا المخزون من أبحاث عن تاريخ فلسطين.

كنت أرى أنه من الضروري تقديم شيء جديد عن فلسطين. يعني هذا ألا نبقى في إطار النص التاريخي السياسي والصراعي وغيره. كنت أبحث دوماً عن الجديد الذي أقدمه لأبناء شعبي عن تاريخه. وهكذا بدأت منذ أن أنهيت المرحلة الثانوية وخلال دراستي الجامعية بإجراء مقابلات شفوية مع كبار في السن في حيفا وعكا وشفاعمرو والناصرة وقرى الجليل. وكان هؤلاء الذين قابلتهم يحكون عن حياتهم قبل وقوع النكبة في 1948، وكيف أنهم كانوا يعيشون في ظروف أفضل بالرغم من أنهم كانوا تحت حكم الانتداب البريطاني. ومنهم من كان يعرض عليّ صوره وصور عائلته التي عكست مشاهد من الحياة العائلية الخاصة والمجتمعية العامة في ذاك الزمن. وآخرون عرضوا علي وثائق قديمة لملكيات أراضيهم وبيوتهم ومحلاتهم التي نهبها المهاجرون الصهيونيون وحرموهم منها.

كل هذه الأمور جعلتني أُفكّر عميقاً بماذا ابدأ. هل أنقل التاريخ الشفوي للناس وعلاقتهم بالمكان الذي ولدوا فيه، أم أتطرق إلى مساهمتهم في بناء مجتمعهم الفلسطيني. في حين أنني كنت أُفكّر أيضاً في الطريقة التي يجب علي عرض هذا التاريخ أو نقله إلى الجيل الحالي كي لا ينسى اصله وتاريخه وماضيه. ومن جمة أخرى، واجهتني كميات كبيرة من الصور التي بدأت تصل إلى يدي في كل مرة أزور فيها عائلة وأطلب أن انظر في البوم العائلة. قليلون جدًّا الذين اعترضوا على طلبي، بل بالعكس كثيرون رحّبوا بفكرة الاطلاع على البوماتهم وفتحها أمامي لنقرأ معا قصص وحكايات العائلة، وعلاقتها بالمكان الذي عاشوا فيها، وشوقهم الدائم إلى تلك الأيام. كثيرون أتاحوا لي الفرصة بأخذ بعض الصور الأصلية لأنهم يعرفون انني سأقوم بضمها إلى مجموعة مقالاتي وأبحاثي التاريخية التي بدأت تنتشر في كتب وفي الصحف المحلية أو من خلال ندوات ومحاضرات أقوم بتنظيمها مع أصدقاء في مدن وقرى مختلفة من فلسطين. هذه المحاضرات أثارت ولا تزالُ تثيرُ الكثيرين للعودة حالاً إلى الالبومات العائلية المتوفرة لديهم ومراجعة الصور القديمة التي لديهم.

لكن يبقى السؤال المركزي هنا، والذي اعتبره عنصراً مكوناً لكل فكرة تجنيد التاريخ الشفوي والصورة الفوتوغرافية لخدمة النص التاريخي، وبالتالي لخدمة الرواية التاريخية الفلسطينية. روايتي انا ورواية شعبي الذي تعرض على مدى أكثر من مائة عام إلى كل أشكال الاقتلاع والطرد والتهجير وإبادة المكان وإبادة الثقافة... كل ذلك في سبيل إقامة دولة لمجموعات بشرية لا صلة بينها، سوى الصلة التي كوّنتها وشكلتها الحركة الصهيونية بالتواطؤ التام مع الدول الاستعمارية الكولونيالية.

ولكني قبل ان أقوم بعملية توضيح هذه العلاقة القوية والفعلية بين التاريخ الشفوي والصورة، بودي توضيح مفهوم التاريخ الشفوي بالنسبة للفلسطيني، لأنه يُسهّل علي القيام بعملية الربط بينها.

يهدف التاريخ الشفوي إلى تثبيت الوجود الفلسطيني في المكان بالرغم من تهجيره واقتلاعه منه. معنى ذلك أن هذا التاريخ، وقد يتحول إلى تاريخ دراسي مبني وفق أسس علمية وموضوعية ومقرون بالقرائن التاريخية، ما هو إلا استعادة الماضي الزمني بكل ما يحويه من مخزون حضاري لتأكيد الحضور الفلسطيني في فلسطين الملموسة أو المتخيلة أو الموعود بها.

فمن هنا يتبين لنا أنَّ التاريخ الشفوي هو الرواية الفلسطينية المُحمَّلة بصور الماضي بعيداً عن مظاهر الخوف الذي سيطر لعدة عقود على الجيل الأول والثاني من النكبة، وكذلك الشعور بالهزيمة والانكسار والعيب والخجل مما حدث. هذا التاريخ فتح المجال أمام الباحثين خاصة والناس عامة لخوضه، لكونه أكثُر سهولة ويُسرًا، إذ فيه تحرير للذات من قيود الخجل والهزيمة والالتصاق بقواعد الكتابة التاريخية البحثية.

وصل عدد اللاجئين الفلسطينيين المسجلين رسمياً في سجلات الأمم المتحدة في شهر ديسمبر من سنة 1949 الى 940,000 لاجئ. وفي نفس السنة قررت الأمم المتحدة تأسيس وكالة الأونروا UNRWA United Nations Relief an Work agency ، وهي وكالة خاصة مكلفة بتقديم الحاجات الغذائية والرعاية الصحية والتعليم للمهاجرين الفلسطينيين. لقد شُكّلت الوكالة للقيام بمهمة مؤقتة "إلى أن يتمكن اللاجئون من العودة الى بيوتهم" . ولكن الجرح الفلسطيني ما زال ينزف إلى يومنا هذا، مما يشكل وصمة عار على جبين للعالم الغربي ، وللمتجمع الدولي. وتحولت نكبة 1948 الى نكبة دائمة.

البروفسور خضر بشارة

جامعة لوفينا الكاثوليكية

هذه الواقعة، وغيرها الكثير، تدحض الدعاية الصهيونية والتي تقول إن الفلسطينيين هربوا من مناطق القتال، وتسلط الضوء على زيف الشعار الصهيوني الذي تكرره منذ سنة 1948 وحتى الآن والقائل إن الجيش الإسرائيلي هو أكثر جيوش العالم أخلاقية.

مما لاشك فيه أن تدمير المجتمع الفلسطيني كان هدفاً مدبراً ضمن ما يمكن تسميته " بالتصفية المجتمعية " " المسح للذاكرة " كما يعترف بذلك موشي ديان في مذكراته إذ يقول:"ليس هناك ضيعة،أو قرية،أو مدنية في إسرائيل باسم عبري لم يكن لها اسم عربي من قبل .. علينا الاعتراف بأننا بنينا بلداً على انقاض العرب "

انطلاقا من القلق الذي شعر به الأمريكيون والفرنسيون حيال تطورات الأحداث الإجرامية التي كانت تجري في فلسطين وخشية منهم مما قد يترتب على ذلك من مخاطر كاندلاع مواجهات عنيفة تعم المنطقة، قدموا اقتراحا للأمم المتحدة بتضمن إرسال مبعوثٍ خاصٍ إلى فلسطين من أجل البحث عن مخرج سلمي للوضع. وتم اختيار الكونت برنادوت Bernadotte، ابن أخ ملك السويد. انتهى المبعوث الأممي برنادوت من إعداد تقريره و صياغته يومي 15 و 16 سبتمبر 1948 وجاء في ذلك التقرير: تلقيت الكثير من التقارير والمعلومات التي تتحدث عن عمليات سطو، وسلب، ونهب، وسرقات، على نطاقٍ واسع، وكذلك عمليات تدمير قرى بدون أي مبرر عسكري. يجب على الحكومة الإسرائيلية المؤقتة أن تضطلع بمسئولياتها بإعادة الممتلكات الخاصة لأصحابها العرب، وتعويضهم عن كل ما تم تدميره بشكل واسع [8] كما أوصى الكونت برنادوت: بمنح منطقة الجليل الغربي للدولة الإسرائيلية، وإلحاق النقب بالدولة العربية، وضم الضفة الغربية إلى الضفة الشرقية، وتدويل القدس "وتمكين اللاجئين الفلسطينيين من العودة إلى بيوتهم" من الواضح أن التوصية الأخيرة غير مقبولة من قبل الدولة الإسرائيلية، فزعماء هذه الدولة عملوا كل ما في وسعهم لإقامة دولة على أسس عرقية يهودية. في اليوم التالي لتقديم التقرير، أي في 17 سبتمبر 1948 تم اغتيال الكونت برنادوت ومرافقه العقيد الفرنسي أندريه سيروت على أيدي جماعة إرهابية يهودية تسمى شتيرن .

اتخذت الجمعية العامة للأمم المتحدة في 11 ديسمبر 1948 القرار رقم 1947 يطالب بتمكين اللاجئين الراغبين بالعودة إلى بيوتهم والعيش بسلام مع جيرانهم، على أن يتم ذلك في أقرب وقت ممكن، كما طالب بدفع تعويضات لأولئك الذين يفضلون عدم العودة على ما فقدوه من ممتلكات أو بسبب الأضرار التي لحقت بهم وبممتلكاتهم بناء على أحكام القانون الدولي التي تحمل السلطات أو الحكومات المسئولة عن هذه التعويضات.

ضرب هذا القرار بعرض الحائط كغيره من القرارات، وعلى الرغم من ذلك وافق السيد بانش خليفة برنادوت على تولي رئاسة مراسيم التوقيع على اتفاقية وقف إطلاق النار بين إسرائيل ومصر في 24 فبراير سنة 1949، وكذلك اتفاقيات مماثلة مع لبنان بتاريخ 23 مارس، ومع الأردن بتاريخ 3 أبريل ومع سوريا بتاريخ 20 يوليو . من الواضح بأن الدول العربية وقعت – من خلال هذه الاتفاقيات - على الاعتراف بهزيمتها العسكرية والسياسية . في نهاية سنة 1949 كانت إسرائيل قد فرضت سيطرتها على 78% من أرض فلسطين التي مزقت وقسمت، وتم تشتيت شعبها في المهجر وفي مخيمات اللاجئين في الضفة الغربية وغزة والأردن ولبنان وسوريا.

كتب مناحيم بيغن ، زعيم عصابة أرغون وبالتالي المسئول الأول عن المذبحة في مذكراته بعنوان (التمرد) يقول: بدون النصر الذي حققناه في دير ياسين لم يكن ليكتب لإسرائيل الوجود[5]، بعبارة أخرى بدون تشريد الفلسطينيين، أي بدون التصفية العرقية، لم تكن إسرائيل لتتولد كدولة يهودية . وبالفعل قبل الإعلان عن قيام دولة إسرائيل، أي قبل اندلاع الحرب العربية الإسرائيليةالأولى أجبر حوالي 300,000 فلسطيني على مغادرة ديارهم نحو الشتات. هذه الحقيقة هي خير دليل على زيف الدعاية الإسرائيلية التي دأبت على الترويج لحجة واهية وهي أن الحرب التي شنها العربُ كانت السبب في كارثة المهاجرين الفلسطينيين.

أبحر السيد آلان كونيغهام، آخر وسابع مندوب سامي بريطاني في فلسطين مساء 14/مايو 1948 على ظهر الباخرة أروالوس عائداً إلى بلاده معلناً بذلك نهاية الانتداب البريطاني على فلسطين. في اليوم التالي 15/مايو 1948 أعلن بن غوريون عن قيام دولة إسرائيل. وبعد 11 دقيقة من هذا الإعلان بالضبط أعلنت الإدارة الأمريكية الاعتراف بالحكومة المؤقتة برئاسة دافيد بن غوريون باعتبارها السلطة الفعلية في الدولة الوليدة للتو.

حاولت الدول العربية، بضغط من شعوبها، إفشال المشروع الصهيوني، ولكن إسرائيل خرجت ظافرة من المواجهة العسكرية ووسعت حدودها باحتلال أراضٍ جديدة، مما ترتب على ذلك المزيد من الشتات الفلسطيني والمزيد من الكوارث. دأبت الدعاية الصهيونية على القول طوال السنوات الماضية بأن اللاجئين الفلسطينيين هربوا من البلاد نتيجة الحروب والمواجهات المسلحة، مستغلةً كارثة الشعب الفلسطيني لخدمة مصالحها، كانت ومازالت هذه الفكرة تُشكّل إحدى القواعد الأساسية للدعاية الصهيونية، بل ذهبت هذه الدعاية إلى حد القول بأنّ زعماء العرب هم الذين نصحوا الفلسطينيين، بل أمروهم بإخلاء بيوتهم والهرب. وقد أصغى الغرب وصدق هذه الدعاية، فالغرب دأب على التعامل مع هذا الموضوع كالأصم الأبكم خلال سنوات طويلة. والواقع هو أن ما جرى في فلسطين لم يكن سوى تصفية مجتمعية ممنهجة، بمعنى آخر تحطيم كامل لمجتمع والشعب. لقد تعامل القادة الإسرائيليون وعلى رأسهم بن غوريون مع هذه الكارثة مستخدمين عبارات اعتبارية "كالنقل القسري" أو "Forced transfer" منذ البداية أي منذ سنة 1940 ومع ذلك عبر جوزيف فيتز مدير الصندوق الزراعي اليهودي عن خطط الصهيونية قائلاً: "علينا أن لا نبقي ضيعة فلسطينية واحدة ولا حتى قبيلة واحدة".

أشارت السيدة كلارا ماريّا دِ أنطونيو في كتابها (تاريخ قضية) إلى وثيقة (الطريق 181) إلى تصريح أدلى به يهودي عمره ثلاثة وسبعين سنة شارك في عملية المكنسة ونقلت عنه القول بافتخار لما قام به من أعمال في شبابه "لقد طردناهم من المنطقة من أجل تحقيق التواصل الجغرافي لأرض إسرائيل. شكلنا سلسلة، وكنا مسلحين جيدا. ننتمي إلى فرقة افتتاح السرية التي تتألف من 1500 رجل... قمنا بملاحقتهم وطردناهم إلى الأردن إلى منطقة ليس بوسعهم العودة منها"[6]

تريسا آرانغورن Teresa Aranguren في كتابها (خيط الذاكرة) تنقل لنا شهادة لاجئ وهو يروي تفاصيل مذبحة طنطورة وهي قرية تقع على الشريط الساحلي إلى الجنوب من مدينة حيفا: "سكان طنطورة معروفون بالعناد، رفضوا مغادرة القرية، عندما اقتحم الجنود اليهود القرية، قاموا بفصل النساء والأطفال ونقلوهم في شاحنة إلى طولكرم. والرجال قسموهم إلى جماعات ووزعوهم على أماكن عديدة داخل القرية وأطلقوا الرصاص عليهم جميعاً"[7].

177

لتفهم أسباب الألم والحزن الفلسطينيين - لذلك القرار - لا بد من الإشارة الى أن اليهود كانوا يمثلون نسبة 33% من السكان ويمتلكون نسبة 6% من الأرض ومع ذلك منحتهم الأمم المتحدة نسبة 56% من الأراضي الفلسطينية. بالإضافة لهذا الظلم السافر قامت جماعات صهيونية مسلحة بعملية تصفية عرقية ممنهجة ومدبرة سلفاً، نفذت في إطار مشروع الدولة ذات الاغلبية اليهودية. وبالفعل في الوقت الذي كانت المنطقة المخصصة للفلسطينيين متجانسة بشريا (725 الف عربي و 10 آلاف يهودي) فإن المنطقة المخصصة للدولة اليهودية كانت تتواجد فيها 272 بلدة عربية و 182 مستوطنة يهودية وعدد سكانها 509.78 عربياً و 499,000 يهودياً. مما يوضح بأن مشروع التقسيم كان يحمل في طياته جنين الكارثة الفلسطينية.

بعد صدور قرار الأمم المتحدة في 29/نوفمبر/1947 شرع زعماء الحركة الصهيونية بحملة منظمة للتطهير العرقي بهدف فرض السيطرة على أوسع مساحة ممكنة وإخلائها من السكان" . أعطى قادة الحركة الصهيونية وعلى رأسهم (بن غوريون) بتاريخ 10/مارس 1948 الضوء الأخضر لتنفيذ خطة Delet والتي حددت الإستراتيجية العسكرية التي يجب انتهاجها من أجل أخلاء البلاد من السكان العرب. ومن بين التعليمات التي وردت في الخطة الفقرة التالية كما نشرها المؤرخ الإسرائيلي إيلان بابيه في كتابه (التصفية العراقية في فلسطين):

يمكن أن تتم العمليات إما بواسطة تدمير القرى (عد حرقها بالنيران أو نسفها بواسطة الألغام التي يجب أن تزرع بين الركام) وبالتركيز على تلك القرى التي يصعب السيطرة الكاملة عليها بشكل مستمر ، أو بواسطة عمليات تمشيط وتحكم طبقاً للتعليمات التالية : تطوق القرى وتجري عمليات التفتيش في داخلها. وفيما إذا وجدت مقاومة مسلحة يجب تصفيتها، وطرد السكان إلى خارج حدود الدولة"[2]

النموذج المتبع عادة يتمثل في مهاجمة القرى الفلسطينية والتنكيل بعدد من السكان وإجبار البقية الباقية على المغادرة وعدم إتاحة اية فرصة لهم للعودة. ويقول المؤرخ الإسرائيلي بني موريس بعبارات واضحة:

"خلال فترة طويلة من سنة 1948 بدأت تتجسد الأفكار المتعلقة بإجبار الفلسطينيين على الهجرة، واتضح على الفور أن تدمير القرى كان الوسيلة الرئيسية لتحقيق هذا الهدف".[3]

وثّق الكاتب الفلسطيني وليد الخالدي عدد القرى الفلسطينية التي دُمّرت خلال الشهور القليلة التي سبقت إعلان قيام الدولة الإسرائيلية والشهور الأولى من الإعلان عن تأسيها بـ 418 قرية، بينما أكدت مصادر أخرى أنّ عدد القرى الفلسطينية التي دمرت أو حُولت إلى كيبوتسات، أو مجاليم أو موشابيم بـ 531 قرية . واضطر (731,000) فلسطينياً تقريباً على الهجرة خلال الفترة من ديسمبر 1947 إلى يونيو 1948.

الفاجعة الأكثر رمزية بدون شك كانت مذبحة دير ياسين، والتي أحدثت موجة عارمة من الذعر في صفوف السكان الفلسطينيين. جرى اقتحام تلك الضيعة القريبة من القدس من قبل قوات أرغون في التاسع من أبريل سنة 1948. كان مندوب الصليب الأحمر في القدس جاك رينير أحد أوائل الشهود الذين وصلوا إلى مسرح المذبحة ويصف المشهد كما يلي :

لقد تم قتل 300 شخص بدون أيّ مبرر عسكري أو استفزاز مسبق. القتلى هم من الشيوخ، والنساء والأطفال، والمواليد الجدد، قتلوا بطريقة وحشية بقنابل يدوية وسكاكين من قبل قوات يهودية من حركة أرغون التي تخضع للسيطرة الكاملة من قبل قادتها.[4]

شترن، وإرغون، وبالماخ، في منتصف الأربعينيات بموجة من العمليات الإرهابية ضد الفلسطينيين والبريطانيين في آن واحد. قامت جماعة إرهابية يهودية تدعى (ارغون زيفاي ليومي) في 22 يوليو سنة 1946 بنسف فندق الملك داوود في القدس وفيه مقر القيادة العامة للجيش البريطاني موقعة أكثر من 90 قتيلا .

على الرغم من العبء الثقيل الناجم عن مرابطة حوالي 100 الف جندي بريطاني (أي جندي واحد لكل 18 مواطنا فلسطينيا) في تلك الفترة، عجزت السلطات البريطانية عن فرض السيطرة على الوضع. واستسلمت للأمر الواقع بتاريخ 18/فبراير/1947، عندما أعلن وزير الخارجية (ارنست بفين) أمام البرلمان قائلا: "قررنا مطالبة الأمم المتحدة بوضع حل"، في الوقت الذي ازدادت فيه مطالب الرأي العام البريطاني بإنهاء المغامرة الفلسطينية تحت شعار (Bring The boys Home) "أعيدوا الشباب إلى بيوتهم" .وبالفعل دُعيت الجمعية العامة للأمم المتحدة في 28/ ابريل 1947 لعقد اجتماع طارئ في Flushing Meadows لدراسة الطلب البريطاني بإنهاء الانتداب على فلسطين.

تصفية المجتمع

اعتبارا من تلك اللحظة بدأت الكارثة تلوح في افق فلسطين: تهجير ثلثي سكان البلاد العرب والذي وصفه البعض (بالتصفية المجتمعية) وهو ما عرفه المؤرخ الفلسطيني صالح عبد الجواد بما يلي: "إنه يعني التدمير الشامل للفلسطينيين، ليس فقط كهوية سياسية أو مجموعة سياسية قومية بل كمجتمع". لتوضيح الإطار العام لهذه الفكرة لا بد من تقديم لمحة تاريخية مختصرة .

احالت بريطانيا القضية الفلسطينية إلى منظمة الأمم المتحدة التي شكلت عدة لجان، وفرق عمل، صيغت عدة خطط ورفضت خطط أخرى مثل : خطة الحكم الذاتي للمحافظات، خطة النظام الفدرالي،والنظام الكونفدرالي ... وأخيراً قررت الجمعية العامة للأمم المتحدة في 1947/09/23 تشكيل لجنة خاصة ad hoc لصياغة الاقتراحات النهائية. وقدم اقتراحان يوصي الاول بتقسيم فلسطين الى دولتين والثاني أوصى بتشكل دولة فدرالية، دولة يهودية ودولة ثنائية القومية. وقد اعتمدت الجمعية العامة للأمم المتحدة في النهاية اقتراح التقسيم بموافقة 25 صوتاً ومعارضة 13 صوتاً وامتناع 19 عن التصويت، البعض منهم قرر التغيب عند التصويت. استخدمت الولايات المتحدة كافة الوسائل من ضغوطات مالية، ودبلوماسية وتهديدات لدول في أمريكا اللاتينية من أجل كسب الدعم لمشروع التقسيم (طالعوا كتابي تاريخ فلسطين أبناء أجينور، أوروبا والفلسطينيون: من الحروب الصليبية وحتى القرن الواحد والعشرين).[1]

استقبل اليهود قرار التقسيم بالغبطة والفرحة بينما انتابت الفلسطينيين مشاعرُ الحزن والصدمة. قسم القرار الأرضي الفلسطينية إلى ستة أجزاء رئيسية : ثلاثة منها (56%من المساحة الاجمالية) لتقام عليها الدول اليهودية والثلاثة الباقية (46%) لتقام عليها الدولة الفلسطينية، بينما تصبح القدس وما حولها (0,65%) منطقة دولية .

النكبة الفلسطينية (1947- 1949): تصفية مجتمع

استخدمت فلسطيني خلال الفترة 1917 الى 1947 كورقة للمراهنة في المناورات الاستعمارية البريطانية. لم تكن نسبة اليهود في فلسطين تتجاوز 6% من السكان سنة 1917 السنة التي صدر فيها وعد بلفور، والذي تعهدت بموجبه بريطانيا بإقامة "وطن قومي لليهود في فلسطين"، وكان اليهود لا يمتلكون إلا نسبة لا تتجاوز 1% من أراضي فلسطين . خلال 26 سنة من الانتداب البريطاني (1922-1948) قلبت موجات المهاجرين الصهاينة المتلاحقة البنية البشرية للسكان في فلسطين رأساً على عقب، لتصبح نسبة اليهود سنة 1947 ما يقرب من 33% من السكان، ومع ذلك بقيت نسبة الأراضي التي كانوا يمتلكونها في حدود 6,6%. هذه الأرقام تبين، بما لا يدع مجالا للشك، الدورَ الحاسم الذي لعبه الدعم البريطاني للحركة الصهيونية، ومع ذلك يجب أن لا ننسى بأن ذلك الدعم لم يكن عملا خيرياً بل بالعكس تماماً. في الإطار العام للأحداث التي شهدتها منطقة الشرق الأوسط بعد الحرب العالمية الأولى، تلاقت أهداف الصهيونية والمتمثلة بالسعي لاستيطان فلسطين، مع الأهداف البريطانية المتمثلة في تأمين قاعدة دعمٍ قريبة من قناة السويس. هذا يعني أن بريطانيا العظمى استخدمت الصهيونية ضمن إستراتجيتها الإمبراطورية.

لكن حقيقةَ الدور البريطاني السيئ للشعب الفلسطيني يجب أن لا يعفي الصهيونية من المسئولية، فقد اتخذ الصهاينةُ قرارهم في أول مؤتمر لهم عقد في بازل سنة 1897 بإقامة دولة يهودية في فلسطين، وكانوا على علم تام بكل ما سيترتب على ذلك القرار من "مسح لهويتها العربية"، وبعبارة أخرى تغييب شعبها كمقدمة لتهويد البلاد، الشعار المزيف الذي رفعه الصهاينة منذ بداية القرن العشرين (أرض بلا شعب لشعب بلا أرض) كان محور الفكر الصهيوني. حايم وايزمن، وهو ما عبّر عنه أحدُ كبار قادة الحركة الصهيونية، إذ اعترف بذلك بجلاء حين قال: "لو اطلع أيُّ شخص على نصوص الوثائق الصهيونية، لما وجد أيَّ إشارة إلى العرب ".

لكن الفلسطينيين موجودون بالفعل، ومتشبثون بأرضهم ويدافعون عنها، كما اثبتت العديد من حركات التمرد ضّد النهج السياسي البريطاني المتواطئ مع المشروع الصهيوني طوال سنوات الانتداب بين الحربين العالميتين. بن غوريون الذي ترأس إسرائيل فيما بعد، أطلق تصريحاً مدهشاً خلال تلك الفترة قال فيه: "الحقيقة هي أننا نحن المتعدون وهم يدافعون عن أنفسهم، فالبلاد بلادهم لأنهم يعيشون فيها، بينما نسعى نحن للتوافد إليها لتثبيت أنفسنا".

لم يكن هدف الحركة الصهيونية مجرد حركة استيطان في الأرض الفلسطينية بل حركة اقتلاع شعبها منها. ولتحقيق هذا الغرض والسيطرة على المجال الفلسطيني، استخدموا كل الوسائل سواء الرمزية أو المؤسساتية أو المالية كما استعملوا، بدون شك، مفاهيم وآليات استعمارية وانعزالية كمبدأ عدم التصرف بالأراضي التي تم السيطرة عليها من قبل اليهود، وعدم السماح للفلاحين الفلسطينيين (سواء كانوا مسلمين أو مسحيين) بمواصلة العمل في هذه الأراضي.

خلال الحرب العالمية الثانية كانت الحركة الصهيونية قد ثبتت موطئ قدم لها في فلسطين، ولكنّ زعماء هذه الحركة كانوا يعلمون جيداً أنّ دور بريطانيا قد أشرف على الانتهاء، وبدؤوا يوجهون أنظار اللوبي الصهيوني نحو الولايات المتحدة. أي أنهم بعد أن حصلوا على الرعاية البريطانيين الكاملة، بدؤوا يشعرون أن هؤلاء تحولوا إلى عقبة في وجه إقامة دولة إسرائيل. عندها قامت الحركات الصهيونية المسلحة كحركة

كان عدد سكان فلسطين في ذلك الحين 1,972,000 نسمة منهم 603.000 ألف يهودي (ثلث عدد السكان) و 47,7% من الأراضي كانت مملوكة من قبل العرب، ونسبة 6,6% مملوكة من اليهود، والنسبة الباقية 46% كانت أراض عامة ومشاعاً . [8]

استحالة قيام الدولة اليهودية إلا من خلال تفريغ الأرض من سكانها العرب.

تريسا أرانغورن

صحـ اف ية

دام الإضراب الذي شلّ معظم النشاطات الاقتصادية والتجارية عمومَ البلاد ستةً أشهر. واستمرَّ التمرّد سنة كاملة، وكانت محصلة القمع البريطاني أكثر من 1000 قتيل فلسطيني و2500 معتقل و54 حكماً بالإعدام شنقاً. بدا وكأنّ هذه الحملة حققت بعض النتائج السياسية. ففي أيّار سنة 1939 أصدرت الحكومة البريطانية الكتاب الأبيض الذي تضمن إعلاناً بالحدِّ من الهجرة الصهيونية وتعهداً بمنح فلسطين الاستقلال خلال عشرة سنوات، اعتبرت الحركة الصهيونية هذا الإعلان تحولاً في سياسة بريطانيا وتهديداً لمشروعها في إقامة وطن لليهود.

على الرغم من تسارع وتيرة شراء الأراضي الفلسطينية من قبل الحركة الصهيونية خلال السنوات العشر السابقة، إلا أن الحركة الصهيونية توصلت إلى قناعة بأنّ من المستحيل تحقيق الهدف المنشود والمتمثل في تحويل اليهود إلى أغلبية في فلسطين وعليه ارتأت بأنّ الحل هو اللجوء إلى العنف.

وقد عبر مدير الصندوق القومي اليهودي جوزيف ويز عن ذلك بوضوح سنة 1940، حيث قال: قامت الصهيونية بنشاطات مثمرة في مجال اقتناء الأرض، ولكننا بهذه الطريقة لن نتمكّن أبداً من إقامة الدولة. فالدولة يجب أن تُمنح لنا دفعة واحدة كعملية إنقاذ. ألم يكن هذا هو سرّ فكرة إعادة بناء الهيكل؟ ليس هناك وسيلة أخرى لطرد العرب، كل العرب. سيتحتّم علينا أن لا ندع قريةً أو تجمعاً سكانياً أو قبيلة عربية في فلسطين، باستثناء بيت لحم والقدس والناصرة. [7]

في هذه الأثناء كانت أوروبا تخوض حربا شرسة، خصصت لها بريطانيا وحلفاؤها كلَّ ما لديهم من طاقات للقتال ضدَّ ألمانيا النازية. ومن البديهي القول بأنَّ مصير الفلسطينيين لم يكن من بين من أولياتٍ أو حتى من مصادر قلق الحكومة البريطانية، وعليه فإنّ التعهدات التي وردت في الكتاب الأبيض لن يُكتب لها التنفيذ أبداً.

بعد تقديم الكتاب الأبيض، الذي يمكن القول بأنّه جاء استجابةً لبعض المطالب الفلسطينية، بدأت المنظمات الصهيونية الأكثر تطرفاً حرباً ضد سلطات الانتداب البريطاني، وشنت سلسلة من الأعمال الإرهابية.

في تموز من سنة 1946 نفذت جماعة صهيونية مسلحة تدعى أرجون تسفاي ليومي عملية نسف فندق الملك داود (كينغ دافيد)، مقر الإدارة البريطانية، مما أدى إلى مقتل 91 موظفاً بريطانياً. وبعد ستة شهور فقط تخلت بريطانيا عن انتدابها على فلسطين، وأحالت ملفَّ المسئولية إلى الأمم المتحدة. في تشرين الثاني من سنة 1947 أصدرت الأمم المتحدة قرار تقسيم فلسطين إلى دولتين: دولة عربية وأخرى يهودية، بريطانيا امتنعت عن التصويت على ذلك القرار. منح قرار التقسيم نسبة 57% من فلسطين التاريخية لإقامة الدولة اليهودية و 43% للدولة العربية.

Diario de Jossef Weitz. Citado por Ilan Halevi en *Sous L´Israel, la Palestine*. Ed Le Sycomore. Paris 1979 [7]

على الرغم من التجانس الواضح بين الإدارة البريطانية والأهداف الصهيونية إلا أن النخبةَ السياسية الفلسطينية والمجتمعَ الفلسطيني ككل كان ما يزال يثق بقدرته على إقناع الحكومة البريطانية بالاستجابة لمطالبه وتخليها عن سياسة التعاون مع الصهاينة. وقد شُكّلت لجانٌ ووفودٌ للسفر إلى بريطانيا مرة تلو الأخرى من أجل شرح مواقفها ومبرراتها وتبليغ حكومة بريطانيا باستياء السكان والتحذير من خطر اندلاع العنف.

في رسالة أرسلت سنة 1921 من قبل سكرتير الشؤون الاستعمارية، السيد ونستون تشرشل، إلى الوفد العربي، رسمت الوضع على النحو التالي:

الاستياء المتزايد في صفوف السكان الفلسطينيين ناجم عن قناعتهم بأن السياسة الحالية للحكومة البريطانية تهدف لطردهم من بلادهم من أجل تحويلها إلى وطن قومي للمهاجرين اليهود. لقد صدر وعد بلفور بدون التشاور معنا، وليس بوسعنا قبول أن يرسموا لنا مستقبلنا.[6]

تفجر الغضبُ الفلسطيني في أغسطس 1929، على إثر مظاهرة قام بها اليهود انتهت برفع العلم الصهيوني على الحائط المبكي، عندها نزل مسلمو القدس إلى الشوارع، وسرعان ما انتشرت الاحتجاجات وعمّت معظم المناطق وتحولت إلى اقتحامات لأحياء يهودية في الخليل وصفد وتل أبيب. نجم عن تلك الاضطرابات مصرع 133 يهوديا و116 عربيا، وألقت الشرطة القبضَ على حوالي ألف شخص (وصدرت أحكام بإعدام 26 شخصاً منهم 25 عربياً ويهودياً واحداً).

الثورة الكبرى

شمل الغليان المعادي للبريطانيين والصهاينة كلّ قطاعات المجتمع الفلسطيني بما في ذلك النساء. عقد المؤتمر الأول للنساء العربيات الفلسطينيات سنة 1932، خلال السنوات اللاحقة عقدت وفود نسائية من المسلمات والمسيحيات اجتماعات مُتكررة مع سلطات الانتداب، وسافرت تلك الوفود النسائية إلى لندن من أجل عرض مطالبهن والمطالب الوطنية بشكل عام.

في منتصف عقد الثلاثينات سادت فلسطين أجواء عصيان عام. وفي أيّار 1936 وجّهت اللجنة العليا العربية، التي كان يرأسها الحاج أمين الحسيني، نداء للعصيان المدني، دعت فيه المواطنين إلى إضراب عام في جميع الأراضي الفلسطينية. وبذلك بدأت حملة الثورة الفلسطينية، الانتفاضة الأولى.

---

[6] رسالة إلى شرشيل بعث بها الوفد العربي الذي زار لندن من أجل التعبير عن المعارضة لإدراج وعد بلفور ضمن شروط الانتداب البريطاني على فلسطين بتاريخ 24 اكتوبر 1921.

في هذه الأجواء المشحونة اندلعت الحرب العالمية الأولى، التي عنت نهاية الإمبراطورية العثمانية، ودخول فرنسا وبريطانيا إلى مسرح الأحداث في المنطقة. هاتان القوّتان الاستعماريتان اللتان كان قد مضى عليها زمن يعملان فيه كحليفتين وحليفتين للقوميّة العربية. في هذا الصدد تبادل المندوبُ السامي البريطاني في مصر (هنري مكماهون) وحسين، شريف مكّة، خلال سنتي 1915 و1916، سلسلةً من الرسائل تعهدت فيها الحكومة البريطانية بالاعتراف وبدعمِ استقلال الولايات السورية عن سيطرة العثمانيين، مقابل تعهد شريف مكة بإعلان الحرب على الأتراك . وهذا ما حصل بالفعل، فقد حارب العرب في صفّ الدول الحليفة وهم على ثقة بأنّهم سيحصلون على استقلالهم بعد أن تضع الحرب أوزارها. لكن في الوقت الذي كان يتعهد فيه مكماهون للشريف حسين بذلك، كانت الحكومة البريطانية تتفاوض سرّاً مع نظيرتها الفرنسية لتقسيم الأراضي العربية بعد التخلص من السيطرة العثمانية. وبالفعل تمّ التوصل إلى اتفاقٍ سُمّي باسم الدبلوماسيّيْن اللذين وقعاه سايكس و بيكو تم بموجبه منح فرنسا السيطرة على سوريا الحالية ولبنان، أما العراق وشرق الأردن (الأردن الحالي) وفلسطين فكانت من نصيب البريطانيين. من الواضح أنّ المصير المأساوي لفلسطين كان قد رُسِم في دهاليز الحكومة البريطانية في لندن.

في نوفمبر سنة 1917 أرسل آرتر جيمس بلفور وزير الخارجية صاحبة الجلالة البريطانية رسالة إلى البارون ليونيل والتر روتشيلد، وعده فيها بدعم بريطانيا العظمى لمشروع إقامة "وطن قومي لليهود في فلسطين"، وعد بلفور الشهير لم يكن سوى رسالة سرية بدون أي قيمة قانونية. لكن الشرعية لم تكن أبداً عاملاً يؤخذ في الحسبان في حالة عرقلتها للمصالح الاستعمارية. وكمثال على النفاق الاستعماري نجده في الفقرة التالية من المذكرة التي أرسلها اللورد بلفور إلى حكومته بلاده سنة 1919.

في فلسطين لن نتخذ الإجراءات الشكلية بـ استطلاع رغبات سكان هذا البلد. فالدول الأربع الكبرى ملتزمة بالاستجابة لرغبات الصهيونية، فالصهيونية سواء كانت على صوابٍ أم على خطأٍ، طيبة أم خبيثة تمتد جذورها في أعماق التقاليد القديمة، والحاجة الراهنة والأمل بالمستقبل، وهذا الأمر أهم بكثير من رغبات وتحفظات 700.000 عربيّ يعيشون في هذه الأرض القديمة. [5]

دخل الجيشُ البريطاني بقيادة الفريق اللنبي القدسَ في التاسع من نوفمبر سنة 1917، بعد استسلام الجيش العثماني. وبقيتنسمة.ن تحت سيطرة القوات البريطانية حتى شهر يوليو 1922. أقرت عصبة الأمم الانتدابَ البريطاني على فلسطين، وشمل الانتدابُ التزام الانتداب بوعد بلفور، أي بإنشاء وطن قومي لليهود في فلسطين .

بلغ تعداد سكان فلسطين طبقاً لإحصاء أجراه الانتدابُ البريطاني سنة 1921 حوالي (762.000) نسمة . منهم 76, 9% مسلمون، و11, 6% مسيحيون، و 0, 9% أتباع معتقدات أخرى., 4%. أما بالنسبة إلى ملكية الأرض فإنّ الحركة الصهيونية لم تكن تسيطر سوى على 2,4% من الأراضي الفلسطينية.

---

[5] خليل السكاكيني شخصية معتبرة من عائلة فلسطينية عريقة. أحد مؤسسي الأكاديمية الدستورية في القدس ، وشخصية مميزة كغيرها من الشخصيات الفلسطينية المسيحية المعتبرة في حركة القوميين العرب .

كانت مُلكية الأراضي في فلسطين على مرّ العصور تنتقل من مالك لآخر، وقد زادت وتيرة انتقال الملكية بشكل لافت في النصف الثاني من القرن التاسع عشر، ولكن المزارعين الذين يزرعون تلك الأراضي كانوا يستقرّون فيها. انقلب الوضع بشكل جذري مع وصول طلائع المستوطنين الصهاينة. فالعائلات التي كانت تفلح الأراضي بموجب نظام التأجير وتبادل العوائد الساري منذ قرون طُردت من أراضيها بعد أن اشتراها الملياردير (البارون روتشيلد)، أو الصندوق القومي اليهودي. تفاقمت هذه الظاهرة وازدادت خطورتها مع بداية القرن العشرين، عندما أصبحت سياسةُ تهويد العمل جزءاً أساسياً من أهداف الحركة الصهيونية.

نموذج عن عقد الصندوق القومي اليهودي يقرّ:

يتعهد المستأجر أن يقوم بكافة الأعمال الزراعية مستخدماً أيادٍ عأن تكوندية حصراً (...) كما يشترط العقد أن لا تُعطى الأرض بغرض فلاحتها لغير اليهود بتاتاً، وفي حال تُوفِّيَ المالك وترك وارثاً غير يهودي فإن للصندوق الحقَّ في استعادة الملكية (...) [3]

بالنسبة للحركة الصهيونية لم يكن شراء الأرض كافياً، بل كان يجب أن تكون خالية من سكانها.

الحرب الكبرى

كانت الأجواء في فلسطين كما في المشرق العربي، خلال السنوات القليلة التي سبقت اندلاعَ الحرب العالمية الأولى، مشحونةً بالتوترات السياسية، وتنامي مشاعرِ القومية العربية ضدّ السيطرة التركية. وفي فلسطين بالذات كانت الأجواء، بالإضافة إلى هذه المشاعر، أكثرَ توتراً بسبب الاستياء المتزايد للفلاحين المحرومين من حقوقهم والغضبِ المتصاعد حيال الأتراك، الذين لم يتخذوا أيَّ إجراء جدّيّ ضدّ زحف الصهاينة. وقد شنت صحيفتان فلسطينيتان، هما صحيفة فلسطين الكرمل وصحيفة الإقدام، خلال الشهور التي سبقت الحربَ، حملةً ضدّ النشاطات الصهيونية، حيث نشرت جريدة الإقدام مقابلة مع المثقف الفلسطيني خليل السكاكيني في آذار سنة 1914 قال فيها:

يسعى الصهاينة للسيطرة على فلسطين، أي على قلب البلاد العربية النابض... إذا أردت أن تقضي على أمّة فاقطع لسانها واحتلّ أرضها، هذا هو بالضبط ما يسعى إليه الصهاينة حيال الأمة العربية. [4]

Idem [3]

لم تكن فلسطينُ ولا بشكلٍ من الأشكال موصودة الأبواب أمام التواصل مع الأجانب. المجتمع الفلسطيني لم يكن مجتمعاً عدوانياً ولا متعصباً دينياً، في تلك الفترة التي وصل فيها الرعيل الأول من مستوطني الحركة الصهيونية. لم تكن تلك الأرض خاليةً من السكان أو صحراء قاحلة كما كانت ومازالت تروّج بعض أبواق الدعاية الفعالة.

نورد فيما يلي الوصف الذي يقوم به اثنان من الرحالة الأسبان (خوسيه ماريا فرناندث سانتشث و فرانسيسكو فريري فيريرو) لمنطقة يافا:

"توجد فيها غابات كثيفة من أشجار الرمان والبرتقال والليمون وقصب السكر والنخيل. حدائقها الرائعة تحتوي على أنواع كثيرة من النباتات، بساتينها تحتوي على كلّ أنواع البقوليات والخضراوات، المروية بمياه نواعير كثيرة. الطبيعة هنا خلابة، تنتشر فيها الحدائق الساحرة، التي ربما تعطي أفضل برتقال في العالم.

وفي سنة 1891 يكتب الكاتب اليهودي الروسي أشِر جينسبورغ، الذي عادة ما يوقّع باسم إحاد هَعام المستعار، على إثر زيارة له قام بها إلى فلسطين:

اعتدنا ، نحن الذين نعيش خارج " إسرائيل"، على الاعتقاد بأن الأرض تكادُ تكون بالكامل قاحلة وجافة وغير مشغولة، وأنّ بوسع من يشاء أن يتملّك أرضاً بدون أيّ عناء. ولكن الحقيقة غير ذلك. من الصعب أن تجد في كلّ البلد أرضاً زراعية بوراً، وحدها المناطق الرملية والجبال الصخرية التي لا تصلح للزراعة بقيت دون فلاحة¹.

لم تكن فلسطين صحراء قاحلة تنتظرُ وصول المستوطنين الأجانب كي تزدهر. كان فيها، كما في المناطق الواقعة بخلاف المزارعين الأبيض المتوسط، مناطق صحراوية ومناطق مشغولة، بعضها خصب للغاية، مشغول بجهد من قبل مزارعين مستقرين فيه منذ أجيال. أما الصحراء فما زالت كما كانت صحراء.

في الحقيقة لم تكن المستعمرات الصهيونية مربحة بحدّ ذاتها، وبقاؤها كان مرهوناً برأسمال روتشيلد ثم بالصندوق القومي اليهودي. كان المستعمرون اليهود الجددُ بخلاف المزارعين المحليين المدينين دائماً، يعتمدون على نوع القروض غير المردودة. هذا ما أوضحه التقرير المتعلق بتوزيع الأراضي الفلسطينيةهو مجردفت الحكومة البريطانية به السير جون هوب سيمسون بإعداده سنة 1930:

الجزء الأكبر من رأس المال اليهودي المُستثمر في فلسطين هو مجرد هدية لا يترتب عليها أيّ فوائد أو مستلزماتٍ مالية مردودة ... وبالنسبة للمستوطنات الزراعية يمكن القول أنه ليس هناك مستوطنة واحدة قادرة على الاكتفاء الذاتي، بمعنى أن تكون قادرة على الاستمرار من دون دعم خارجي².

---

¹ حقيقة أرض إسرائيل لمؤلفه *Verdad de la Tierra de Israel,* Ehad Ha´am Cit por Ilan Halevi en Sous L´Israel, La Palestine, Ed. Le Sycomore. París 1979

² السيد جون هوب سيمسون تقرير عن الهجرة Sir John Hope Simpson: *Report on Inmigration, Land Settlement and Development in* Palestine. 1930

فلسطين: القضية المغيبة

يبدو أنّ اسمَ فلسطين الذي ننطق به كما ننطق اسم إيطاليا أو البرتغال أو العراق، أو القوقاز أو شبه الجزيرة الإيبيرية، فُرِّغ من معناه، كما لو أنّه موجود أو وجد كمشكلة أو صراع أو كحدّ أقصى كوجه آخر مزعج لدولة إسرائيل. لكن فلسطين، قبل أن تتحول إلى مشكلة، كانت ببساطة فلسطين وهذا شيء واضح، لكنّه شيء واضحٌ منسيٌّ. وهذا النسيان ليس عرضياً بل هو مُبرمج.

مصطلحُ فلسطينَ وُجدَ في مخطوطات مصرية يرجع تاريخها للقرن الثاني عشر قبل الميلاد، وهو الاسم الذي ظل يشير على امتدادِ قرونٍ إلى بقعةٍ من الأرض لها حدودُها الجغرافية وهويتُها الثقافيةُ والاجتماعية، وجغرافيتها البشرية، ونظامُها الإداريُّ والسياسيّ. تمتد حدودُها بين البحر الأبيض المتوسط غرباً ونهر الأردن شرقاً، وبين جبال الجليل شمالاً وصحراء سيناء جنوباً. هي أرض اكتسبت هويَّتها المُميَّزة إبّان العهد الروماني وأُطلق عليها اسمُ فلسطين، وظلّت هذه التسمية سارية بدون انقطاعٍ حتى القرن التاسع عشر، عندما شكلت جزءاً من الولاية السورية التابعة للإمبراطورية العثمانية، ومع ذلك احتفظت باسمها. تاريخُ هذا البلد العريق هو تاريخُ البشرية ككلّ، مَهدُ الأديان وبداية التأريخ للعالمين الشرقي والغربي، والأهم من ذلك كلِّهِ هو أنّ فلسطينَ هي الأرض التي يقطنُها الفلسطينيون.

يمكن القول بأن المشكلة العربية الإسرائيلية قديمة لكنها ليست أزلية أو غابرة في أعماق الزمان، ولا هي مطبوعة في الجينات الوراثية لأهلها، بل لها تاريخ ميلاد وأبوين مُعترف بها.

بدأت القضية مع نهاية القرن التاسع عشر، دون أن يعلم سكانها بأنّ حياتهم ومصيرهم المشترك اكتسبا بعداً إشكالياً، عندما تحولت فلسطين إلى "القضية الفلسطينية"، المشروع الصهيوني الذي بدأ يتشكّل في مكاتب وزارات الخارجية الأوروبية، لم يرسم مستقبلاً غير مُتوقعٍ لسكان فلسطين العرب وحسب، بل كان عليه أن يطمس ماضيهم حتى يُحوِّله إلى مجرد عتبةٍ للدولة اليهودية القادمة.

وصل أوائل مستوطني الحركة الصهيونية إلى أرض فلسطين في العقد الثامن من القرن التاسع عشر، بالتحديد اعتباراً من سنة 1880 عندما كانت المنطقة ما تزال تخضعُ للحكم العثماني، استوطن هؤلاء المهاجرون في السهل الخصب المحاذي للشاطئ، إلى الشمال من يافا، في أراضٍ اشتراها البارون إدموند روتشيلد —الذي لعب دوراً مركزيا في تمويل وتشجيع الهجرة اليهودية- قسم كبير من هذه المشتريات تمّ مستغلاً قوانين مُلكية الأرض التي كانت قد سنتها الإدارة العثمانية سنة 1876 والتي مكنت بعض الإقطاعيين المقيمين في اسطنبول وبيروت من استغلال فرص المتاجرة العقارية المربحة، من خلال الاستيلاء على أراضي وجهاء فلسطينيين عجزوا عن تسديد الضرائب المُجحفة التي كانت تفرضها الإمبراطورية العثمانية عليهم، كي يبيعوها فيما بعد بأسعارٍ مغريةٍ لعملاء روتشيلد وجمعية الاستعمار اليهودي.

في تلك الفترة لم يكن توافد الأوربيين للعيش في الديار المقدسة أمراً مستغرباً. فمنذ منتصف القرن هاجرت مجموعات من المتدينين المسيحيين واليهود إلى فلسطين بدوافع دينية. كما وصلت جاليات من جمعية فرسان الهيكل الألمانية إلى البلاد واستقرّ أفرادُها في حيفا ويافا والقدس ومدنٍ أخرى من المنطقة، وكذلك وفدت عائلات من السويد وأمريكيا، شيدوا بناية جميلة للغاية في القدس — فندق أمريكان كولوني الحالي - هذه مجرّد أمثلةٍ على البصمات التي خلفتها موجةُ المهاجرين المتدينين في المنطقة.

تنهض هذه المجموعة العظيمة من الصور المجموعة هنا ضامة نصوصاً كتبها ثلاثة عارفين رائعين بالقضية الفلسطينية، ويتميزون إضافة إلى ذلك بصرامتهم الفكرية وبوجدانهم الأخلاقي العالي. هي بالنتيجة نصوص

متكاملة فيما بينها   فكل واحد من مؤلفيها يطرح ويُحلّل الموضوعَ انطلاقاً من تجربته الشخصية الخاصّة وقدرتهم المهنية. كذلك تمثل ثلاث طرق لعيش الحالة الفلسطينية والإحساس بها متمايزة خارجياً —لكنّها متلاحمة

ومترابطة بشكل حميم أيضاً-   وبشارة خضر، فلسطيني "من الخارج"، من المنفى، جوني منصور، فلسطيني "من الداخل" ولذلك هو من منفيي الداخل وترسا أرانغورين،

إسبانية صارت فلسطينية بعمق في حياتها وعملها. حافظت معها ومع بشارة منذ سنوات كثيرة ليس على صداقة راسخة وحسب بل وعلى ارتباط طويل وأيضاً راسخ بالقضية الفلسطينية وأهلها. بالنسبة لي كتابة هذه

الصفحات تمنحني فرصةً جديدة لأؤكّد لهما صداقتي وإعجابي. أيضاً تسمح لي بأن أُكتشفَ حساسيةً وتجربةً ساندرا بارّيلارو المهنية اللتين كانتا أساسيتين في اختيار المادّة التصويرية.

*   *   *   *   *   *   *

كثيراً ما أذكر حين أُكتبُ أو أتحدّثُ عن فلسطين ما أكَّدَهُ منذ سنواتٍ أحدُ أكثر الكتاب الفلسطينيين المعاصرين تمثيلاً للقضية، رشاد أبو شاور: "القضيّة الفلسطينية أكثر من مسألة حدود، إنّها مسألة وجود"

هنا المفتاح: لا تتعلّق المسألة بشعبٍ فلسطيني موجود، بل وُجِدَ، وسيبقى موجوداً. وهذا الوجود لا يتطلّب مسكناً، بلداً فقط، بل يتطلّب وطناً، دولة اسمها هكذا: فلسطين. إنّ اللعب السياسي القذر لا يستطيع أن

يزم الواقع النظيف للوجود، كما لا يمكنه الاستمرار بنسيانه، تهميشه، إخفائه. الوجودُ ليس قناعاً ولا يمكن أن يُقَنّع. إنكارُ الوجود إنكارٌ للحياة: أي أنه نوع من الجريمة. جريمة بُدئ باقترافها منذ أكثر من قرن وما زالت

تُقترَف حتى الآن —بطرق أخرى وأقنعة أخرى-. إنّ جريمةً تَستمِرّ دون مُحاكمة ودون حكم بحقّها. هذا ما تُذكّر به وتؤكّدُه هذه الصور.

بِدرو مارتينِثْ مونتابِثْ
أستاذ فخري، جامعة أُوْتُونوما، مدريد.

يعود مضمونه إلى "الزمن السابق" الطويل، إلى الزمن الحاسم، الذي عادة ما يُبقى عليه مخفياً ومجهولاً، كُبعدٍ ومُقصى ، بل هذا هو مقصى عن أرضه، لأنّه انتزعت منه الأرض. على امتداد المرحلة المنقضية ما بين العقود الأخيرة من القرن التاسع عشر والنصف الأوّل من القرن العشرين. تُشكّل التناقض القاسيّ وغير المعهود للزمن الذي لم يمرّ، بالمحصّلة "اللازمن". هل هناك ما هو أقسى وغير إنساني من إنكار الزمن؟ أسمح لنفسي أن أنصحَ وأُثمّن كلّ شخص يقرأ هذا الكتاب –أو يتأمّل محتواه، لأنّها كتابة "تدخل أيضاً عبر العيون" أن يرافق هذه القراءة أو هذا التأمّل بهذه الفكرة الكامنة والأساسية: إنّه يستعيد زمناً، ماضياً أريد له ألا يكون قد مرّ، ألا يكون قد وُجد.. هذا سيُقدم له التوضيح الرئيسي، الذي بقي زمناً طويلاً مخفياً، للقضية الفلسطينية المأساوية، لتاريخ هذا الشعب المعاصر، المأساويّ، الذي لم يعتق بعد.

هذا الكتاب واسع في جوهره ويضم كمية كبيرة من الصور، ألبوم صورٍ استثنائي، محمّل بمعنى عميق جدّاً وأصيل –من أصل-. ونظراً لكونه مجموعة من الصور هو أيضاً شهادة صامتة بقدر ما هي واضحة لشيء متخيّل. يستطيع القارئ أن يتصوّر كالمشاهد لفيلم سينمائيّ وثائقيّ، لتتالي صور، لأطرٍ ولحظاتٍ وحالاتٍ ، هي بالنسبة إليه جذّابة بقدر ما هي مجهولة، جديدة بقدر ما هي غير متوقّعة. لهذا بالضبط هي مُظهِرة قبل كلّ شيء، أي أنّها تكشف له شيئاً كان يجهله جهلاً شبه تامّ، "تُظهره"

يقال عادة إنّ الصورةَ تساوي أكثرَ من ألف كلمة، واحدة من جمل كثيرة تُوضح الكثير وتُقدم طرقاً للمعرفة، لكنّها أيضاً حين تُفهم وتُنادى في تطبيقها فإنّها تنتقص جزئياً من قيمة الأحداث، إنّها صائبة، بلى، لكن أيضاً يمكن أن يُبالغ ويُغطي. الصور والكلمات قيمتها في ذاتها وليس عليها أن تتبادل التنابذ. وبالتالي إذا جاءت معاً ومجتمعة فهذا أفضل.

الصورة هي دائماً بحدّ ذاتها شيء ذو قيمة، لكنّ قيمتها تزداد عندما يُرافقُ نشاطَ المشاهدة الماديّة شيئان آخران: "الرؤية" العقلية والرؤية "الحسّية". بهذه النظرة الثلاثية، بهذا السبيل الثلاثي للنفوذ، يحقّقُ الشيءُ المتأمَّلُ مداه كاملاً، قيمته العليا ومعناه الكامل. أسمح لنفسي أن أرجو عبرَ هذه السطور أن نخصّ هذه المجموعة من الصور الرائعة بهذه الطريقة من الرؤية الثلاثية والواحدة في آن معاً: أن تُركِّز العين والعقل والشعور وتتوحَد في النظرة، أن تكون النظرة متكاملة.

هذا التمرين على النفوذ الثلاثي والمجدول يقودنا لأن نستحضر مثلاً، بين أشياء كثيرة أخرى، أن هؤلاء الكائنات البشرية التي تتأمّلنا بثبات –تتأمّلنا بثبات أكبر حتى من ثباتنا في تأمّلهم- كانت تقطن بلداً ليس واسعاً –أكثر من 20000كم2 بقليل- حيث كان يعيش –بل "يعيش" بكل ما في الكلمة من معنى- قرابةُ المليون نسمة. لا أذكر هذه الأرقام التقريبية بهدف الكمّ والمقارنة، بل بالضبط بهدف معاكس: نوعيّ وأساسيّ. ونتساءل: كيف كان أنّ هؤلاء السكان، المحدودين عدداً ومكاناً ، كانوا متنوعين ومختلفين وأغنياء ومتعدّدين في مظاهرهم وسلوكهم وعاداتهم وحياتهم ولباسهم، في عاداتهم، في طرقهم المتعددة في الحياة والمعاناة والاستمتاع؟ كيف يمكن لفلسطين أن تكون في الوقت ذاته فريدة ومتعدّدة، وخاصّة ومتنوّعة وبسيطة، بساطات كثيرة مختلفة؟ هل كان ضرورياً كسر كلّ هذا، تدميره، تبديله، كي يُعاد لاحقاً بناؤه بعد أن شوّه، حُوّلا، طردا واستبدل؟ ألم يكن هؤلاء الناس يستحقون أن يستمرّوا بالعيش –نعم، هذا هو "بالعيش" كما تبيّن هذه الصور أنّهم كانوا يعيشون؟. ربّما كان هذا هو السؤال الرئيسي، الأقسى والأعمق الذي تسألنا إياه تلك العيون التي تنظر إلينا بثبات، ولا تتوقّف عن النظر إلينا وستبقى تنظر إلينا حتى نكون قد مررنا على كلّ صفحات هذا الكتاب.

لا أريد أن أستمرّ في طريق الاستذكار الشخصي، لكنّي أيضاً لا أتنصّلُ من تقديم معلوماتٍ توثيقية ذات صلة، لِما فيها من دلالة عظيمة ذات علاقة بكلِّ ما أثرته حتى هذه الساعة. كان نحو عام 1967 أتَي بدأتُ بالتعاون الرائع مع صديقي الطيّب الشاعر الفلسطيني محمود صبح، الذي وصل إلى مدريد من دمشق كي يتوسّع في دراساته ويحصل على الدكتوراه، مختاراتٍ مستفيضة للشعر الفلسطيني الحديث جدّاً والمسمى بشعر "المقاومة". وكان قد ظهر للتوّ كتابُ غسان كنفاني الموحي باللغة العربية حول الموضوع وهذا العمل وذاك حول المادّة لمؤلفين آخرين من ذات المنطقة اللغوية. ما إن انتهينا من عملنا الجديد حتى شرعنا بمهمّة البحث عمّن ينشره. كان الموضوع، كما أقول، يُشكّل جِدّةً مطلقةً في المشهد الأدبي الغربي وليس الإسباني فقط. كانت مختاراتنا أوّلَ كتابٍ بلغة أوروبية حول الموضوع. فقط أريدُ أن أُضيف معلومة واحدة: "أضاعوا" لنا في عددٍ من دور النشر —بعضُها معروف بنزعته وتوجّهه"التقدميين"- النسخةَ التي تركناها لهم. بالنتيجة: استطعنا نشره في عام 1969، بفضل المساعدة التي قدّمها لنا معهدٌ أنشئ في ذلك الوقت، واستمرّ بفضلِ راعي آدابٍ من أصل تونسيّ، كان يُسمى البيت الإسباني-العربي. بقيت هذه الأشياء تحدث في هذا البلد "المحبّ جدّاً للعرب".

* * * * * * *

إذا كنتُ قد بدأتُ كما فعلت فهذا لم يكن فقط لأن الأمورَ التي عرضتها تمثل بالتمام الظاهرةَ التي كنت أندّد بها: قطع الرأس المُتعَمَّد -"جزُّ الرأس"- والاجتثاث —الاقتلاع من الجذر- الذي عانت منه القضية الفلسطينية بالتحديد وكلّ ما له علاقة بفلسطين بعامة، لزمن طويل، طويل جدّاً. قصداً وعمداً كانت القضية الفلسطينية بلا أصل، بلا سوابق، بلا بدايات، أو أن هؤلاء كانوا يُعتبرون زائدين عن الوجود وتأفهين يمكن الاستغناء عنهم، لأنّهم كانوا سطحيين، لا يوضّحون ولا يساهمون في توضيح ما حدث بعد ذلك. إن تاريخ القضية الفلسطينية مليء بإهانات الحقيقة وبالجرائم ضدّ الذاكرة. أي أنّه مليء —موبوء- بالجرائم ضدّ الإنسانية.

بدأت كما فعلتُ لأنّ ذلك يسمح لي بتأكيد وإبراز إحدى القيم الأساسيةِ للكتابِ الذي أُقدّم له، إبراز كما تستحق حقيقة إحدى أبرز خصائصه. بهذا المعنى هذا الكتاب يواجه جذرياً وبجسارة واقتدار وصلابة واعتدال كلَّ تلك الكتابات التاريخية المشوِّهة عن عمدٍ والمضلِّلة أو ببساطة الجاهلة في جزء كبير منها، التي راحت تتراكم حول الموضوع. يُركّز هذا الكتبُ بالضبط على إنقاذ وإبراز الكثير من بداياتِ وأصول، وسوابق القضية الفلسطينية.

فاتحة

إنّ تاريخَ المسألة الفلسطينية موبوء بالنسيان، بالخداعِ والتزييف، بالنفاق والتحريف، مليء بالخوف والتباينات والتناقضات والمفاجآت، إلى جانب المآسي والفجائع المستمرة التي تهزّها. ساهم هذا لزمنٍ طويل وفي جوانبَ وأبعادٍ كثيرة في جعلهِ أقرب إلى "معاداة التاريخ"، محاكاةٍ ساخرة له، تاريخٍ مزوّر لا يكاد يشبه في شيء ما يحدث في الواقع، تاريخ شبه احتيالي. امتدّت هذه الحالة عقوداً وكلّف البدء للخروج منها جهوداً هائلة: هكذا بدأ يحدث منذ أكثر من نصف قرنٍ بقليل. قبل أن نتابع، سأسمح لنفسي بتوضيحٍ ومعترضة: استخدمتُ في بداية هذا النص كلمة "موبوء" بكلّ قصدية ومعناها الأول والخاص، لأنّ ما كان يحدث عند كتابة تاريخ المسألة الفلسطينية كان وشكّل هذا بالضبط: وباء حقيقيّ، فاجعة عامّة، مصيبة، محافظاً بذلك وبأعلى درجة على المفهوم التاريخي الأصلي لـ" القرحة"[1].

ربّما كان يتعذّر تفسير هذا العمل في إسبانيا أكثر من بلدانٍ أخرى، ولكي نعطي مثلاً سوف ألجأ إلى ما هو أقرب إليّ ومعرفتي مباشرة أكثر، إلى تجربتي الشخصية ذاتها. درستُ في كلّيةِ الفلسفة والآداب في مدريد، خلال النصف الأول من العقد الخامس من القرن الماضي، اختصاصيْن، وحصلتُ على إجازة من قسم التاريخ (1955) وعلى أخرى من قسم فقه اللغات السامية (1956). خلال دراستي لا أحد —بحسب ما أتذكّر- قام بأدنى إشارة إلى القضية الفلسطينية، وأنا أشير بالتحديد إلى هيئة المدرسين الأكفّاء. طبعاً في برنامجِ دروس التاريخ كان هناك مواد تهتمّ بالمرحلةِ المعاصرة وحتى في قسم الدراسات السامية كان هناك مادة تحملُ بالضبط عنوان: تاريخ الإسلام المعاصر. حسن، ما من ذكر للموضوع الفلسطيني. كان برنامج دراسات ذلك القسم يضمّ مادّة أخرى، ذات مضمون عام، اسمها تاريخ شعب إسرائيل. لا أتذكّر أنّ أحداً فيها قام بأيّ إشارة إلى الحدث الفريد الذي وقع في عام 1948: تأسيس دولة بهذه الاسم ذاته؛ على أرض فلسطين، كما هو معروف.

كلّ هذا حدث في أوّلِ وأهمِّ جامعةٍ إسبانية، في بلد، في كان يُرَدّد فيه الخطاب الممجوج " للعلاقات الإسبانية العربية الأخوية"، كان نظامه يتباهى "بسياساتٍ –عملية- مناصرة للعرب"، وستتأخّر حكومته سنوات كثيرة في إقامة علاقاتٍ دبلوماسية مع هذه الدولة بطابعها الجديد، المؤسسة في 1948. ومع ذلك فكلّ ذلك الذي أحكيه لا يكشف عن جديد، بل هو بالنتيجة واحدة من المعلومات الكثيرة التي تبرهن على شيء نعرفه جيّداً ونعاني من نتائجه وتأثيراته الخطيرة منذ القدم: في هذا البلد، الخاص جدّاً، في إسبانيا لا تتبع السياسةُ والمجتمعُ والثقافةُ عادةً مساراتٍ مُتقاربة. وكم يُلاحظ هذا ويُفْتقد!

بدأتُ أسمع عن فلسطين خلال وجودي في مصر بين بداية 1957 وأواسط 1962 على امتداد وكثافة تجربة القاهرة. وكان أيضاً أن سافرنا أنا وزوجتي مرسيدس إلى الأراضي الفلسطينية، التي كانت تُشكّل وقتذاك جزء من المملكة الأردنية الهاشمية. كان الحدث الفلسطيني واحداً من المستجدات الكثيرة الكاشفة التي راحت تتفتّح أمامي وساهمت بشكل حاسم كي تتوجّهَ حياتي ذاتها، وليس فقط نشاطي المهني كمستعرب، نحو أبعادٍ كانت حتى ذلك الوقت مجهولة تماماً بالنسبة إليّ وتسلك طرقاً هي حتى هذه اللحظة مستغلقة.. الآن وبعد سنوات كثيرة أستطيع، وعليّ أن أعترف، بصفوٍ مطلق وموضوعيةٍ واعتزاز أنّ ذلك استحقّ المُعاناة. إنّ ارتباطي بالقضية الفلسطينية بالتالي بدأ وقت ذاك ولم يفعل شيئاً آخر سوى أنه راح ينمو ويتطوّر ويتنوّع حتى الساعة، محافظاً دائماً ومؤكّداً التزامي الفكري والإنساني بهذا الشعب وبالدفاع عن حقوقه وتطلعاته المشروعة.

---

[1] أصل كلمة وباء في اللغة الإسبانية.

المهمّ أن نسأل من كان خلف العدسة؟ ما الّذي يمكن أن نقوله عن أولئك الّذين عاشوا خارج إطار الكاميرا؟ أين نبحث عن إرثهم؟ إن اللّوحة الّتي يرسمها هذا الكتاب بصوره الفوتوغرافيّة الّتي لم نرها من قبل منوّرة بقدر ما هي غير مكتملة.

إنّ هذا الكتاب واحد من بين الكثير من المشاريع الّتي تسعى إلى توثيق قصصنا وقصص أجدادنا. ولا يزال أمامنا مسؤوليّة كبرى، تبدأ بأحاديث مؤلمة مع أجدادنا قبل أن يتوفّاهم القدر، وتستمر إلى أن نضمن أنّ ضحايا ومقاومي نكبة اليوم ليسوا مجرّد عناوين أخبار عابرة.

يؤكّد كتاب "ضدّ المحو" بأن التّاريخ الفلسطيني لا يبدأ بالهروب. يتحدّى هذا الكتاب التّحريف العنيف الّذي تقوم به الإمبراطوريّات، ومرتزقتها من رجال السياسة والبلطجة، الّتي تسعى إلى دحرنا، ه. ويتحدى الكتاب أيضًا الهندسة الثّقافيّة والسّياسيّة الّتي أخفت النّكبة، وجعلتها غامضة وشائكة وروّجت لرواية تدّعي أن إنهاء النّكبة محال بعيد المنال.

ومع ذلك، تنكر المؤسّسات الإعلاميّة والسياسيّة والأكاديميّة في العالم الغربي هذا التّاريخ الدمويّ وتخفيه. لقد غيّب آباء الصّهيونيّة الأوائل وجودنا منذ اللّحظة الأولى الّتي بدأوا فيها البحث عن قوّة امبرياليّة عظمى تتبنّى مشروعهم في فلسطين. فقبل أن ينكروا المجازر الّتي ارتكبوها بحقّنا، كانوا في الحقيقة ينكرون وجودنا أصلًا. زعمت السّرديّة الاستعماريّة أن فلسطيننا، المتنوّعة المناخ والمنبت، هي في الواقع أرض جرداء "يلا شعب" [3]. وإن حصل أن تواجد بين أشواكها وسهولها القاحلة ناس فعلًا، فهم، على حد قول جابوتنسكي، "همجيّون"، بلا جذور، رُحَّل. قالوا "[أنتم] بقيّة أمّة منشورة بين المغاور" [4]. وهكذا عرفت النّكبة وكأنّها هديّة منحتنا إياها الصهيونية، بدل أنها أكبر عمليّة سطو مسلّح في تاريخ البشريّة الحديث. يجلس اللّصوص ببجاحة في غرف جلوسنا، ويطيلون الزّيارة. يحلبون معزانا ويزرعون البندورة الكرزيّة في بساتيننا. لقد جعلوا الصّحراء تزهر و"حرّر[وا] حتّى السّائمات غداة أن [أعطوا] أبراهام حقل محمّد" [5].

إنّ هذه الأساطير الاستعماريّة كانت ضروريّة لنجاح هذه الحالة المتطرّفة من الهندسة الإجتماعيّة. ولا تزال هذه الأساطير شرط لاستمراريّة المشروع الاستيطاني في فلسطين. يمكنني أن أجزم أن جميع الفلسطينيّين يدركون أن النّكبة لم تكن كارثة مفاجئة ولا ماض مغبر، إلّا أنّني أقلق أحيانًا من أن يتمّ معالجة النّكبة كما لو أنّها حدث يتّسم بالفقدان، ولا شيء غير الفقدان. إنّ القصّة الّتي تقول بأنّنا هربنا بلا قتال تؤكّد أيضًا على فكرة المشروع الاستيطاني الصّهيوني كشيء حصين، وأن مقاومته كانت بلا جدوى وستظلّ بلا جدوى. ولكن لطالما كان المقاومون الفلسطينيّون شوكةً في حلوق المستعمرين، يقاتلون حتى الطلقة الأخيرة، كما يفعلون في نابلس وجنين وغزة، فنحن لم نهزم بعد، ولم ينه المشروع الصّهيوني مهمّته على أرضنا.

قبل أن أكتب هذه الفقرات لمقدّمة الكتاب، سؤال واحد اجتاحني وأنا أقلب بين الصور: ماذا فعلوا بك؟ ماذا فعلوا بفلسطين؟ لقد صدمتني صور فلسطين قبل الجدران والمستوطنات، قبل أن تسدّ الحواجز شرايينها، صور التُقِطَت بين بلدات وقرى يفصل بينها الآن جدران اسمنتية جعلتها عوالمًا مختلفةً تمامًا، فيما كانت في السّابق متّصلةً اجتماعيًا واقتصاديًا. من النّادر أن تصادف أعيننا فلسطين قبل الكيان الاسرائيلي. فلسطين الّتي لا تُعرِّفَها أوجاعها بل صناعاتها وثقافاتها. مع ذلك، لا أريد أن أرسم صورة رومانسيّة لتلك الحقبة، بل أريد قراءتها في سياقها الاجتماعي والسياسي. ولهذا من

---

3 Israel Zangwill, *The Return To Palestine* (1901)

4 راشد حسين، "الله لاجئ"

5 قرأ راشد حسين هذه القصيدة في مؤتمر جمعيّة المزارعين العرب في عكّا احتجاجاً على القانون الإسرائيلي الّذي صدر عام ١٩٦٠ "قانون الأراضي" والّذي صنّف ٩٣٪ من الأراضي في فلسطين التّاريخيّة كأراضي تعود ملكيّتها للدّولة. تشير القصيدة أيضًا إلى قانون أملاك الغائبين ١٩٥٠ والّذي منح الحكومة الإسرائيليّة حق الاستيلاء على ممتلكات اللّاجئين الفلسطينيّين خلال النكبة.

مقدمة

أكتب هذه المقدّمة بالعربيّة وبالإنجليزيّة، وفي هذه اللّحظات بالذّات يظهر الشّرخ العميق بين اللّغتين: ففي اللّغة الإنجليزيّة، هناك حاجة بأن أصبغ الصّفحة بأرقام وحقائق وتواريخ تُفصِّل ملابسات جرائم وجب الاعتراف بها دوليًّا، لا بل واجبٌ منذ عقودٍ طويلة. أجد نفسي على وشك أن أقحم بين هذه السّطور درس تاريخ يعدّد الجماعات الإرهابية الّتي شكّلت الجيش الّذي يرهبنا اليوم؛ كما أعداد المجازر واللّاجئين والمنفيّين؛ والأرقام الّتي لا تحصى لدونمات الأراضي المسروقة؛ وبطون الحوامل الّتي بُقرت في دير ياسين.

لا تتملّكني نفس الغريزة في العربيّة، فلا داعي لشرح السّياق؛ النّكبة تلاحقنا كظلّنا، تجتاح هويّتنا الوطنيّة، وتقتحم وعينا الأوّل لأنفسنا. لا تكلّ. هي فعل مضارع، يحصل في كل مكان على الخارطة. بدأت النّكبة عند بعض العائلات يوم هُجِّر جدٌّ من يافا ليجد ملجأ في غزّة، واستمرّت هناك في القطاع المحاصر، تحت سخط القنابل وضجيج الصّواريخ، لتعرِّفُ أحفاده على حربهم الأولى—أو الثّالثة، أو السّادسة حتّى. لا بقعةٌ من جغرافيّتينا تنفذ منها، ولا جيلٌ [1].

تلاحقنا النّكبة حتّى في المنفى. فأيّ فلسطينيّ ولد في مخيّم عين الحلوة في لبنان، مثلًا، بدلًا من وطن جدّيه عكّا، القريب جدًّا والبعيد أكثر، سيحيا معذَّبًا باحتمالاته المجهضة، بدون مواطنة أو حتّى الحق في التّنقّل. وهي غريبة جدًّا... لا يحتاج المستوطن اليوم إلّا لمسدّس ولهجة أمريكيٍّ ليفلت من تهم جنائيةٍ تلاحقه في الولايات المتّحدة ويختبئ في دفء بيتٍ مقدسيٍّ في حيٍّ من أحياء المدينة، ويستولي عليه بدعم من الجيش والقضاء وطبعاً الله...سمساره المفضّل [2].

---

1 حين بدأت في كتابة هذا النّص في تمّوز ٢٠٢٣، كان جيش الاحتلال يجبر مئات من الفلسطينيّين على الخروج من منازلهم في مخيّم جنين، الّذي كان ليلتها يواجه أكبر حصار عسكري منذ سنة ٢٠٠٢، واستهدفت كتيبة إسرائيليّة العائلات والبنية التحتيّة وطواقم الإسعاف والمقاومين. كان المشهد يشبه بشكل مخيف مشهدا آخر من نيسان ١٩٤٨ حين هُجِّر الآلاف من بيوتهم في حيفا، ووضعتهم الهاغانا في باصات نقلتهم إلى مخيّم جنين، الّذي أصبح بشكل قسريّ مأواهم الجديد.

2 و(للمرّة الثانية، وأنا أكتب هذا النّص، يقف صب لبن أمام منزله الّذي استولى عليه المستوطنين اليهود في البلدة القديمة، ويصيح، "نريد أثاثنا!" وينظر إليه المستوطنون شامتين من علوّ نوافذ بيته، الّذي يسكنوه بلا احراج بين ذكرياته وممتلكاته الشخصية.)

194

كفاني أظلُّ بحضنها

كفاني أموت على أرضها
وأُدفن فيها
وتحت ثراها أذوب وأفنى
وأُبعثُ عشبًا على أرضها
وأُبعث زهره
تعيث بها كفُّ طفلٍ نمته بلادي
كفاني أظلُّ بحضن بلادي
ترابًا
وعشبًا
وزهره

فدوى طوقان، شاعرة فلسطينية، ولدت عام 1914 في نابلس، حيث عاشت حتى وفاتها في عام 2003.

شُكر

صدرَهذاالكتاب بمساعدةٍ كريمةٍ لِعديدٍ من الأشخاص ،فقد جاءَ التشجيعُ من صديقتنا سهيلة عطوان ،وهي فلسطينية تُقيم في مدريد ،بحيث سَهلتْ لنا الاتصال مع البروفسور منصور وافرادِ عائلته في حيفا.وخلال زيارتنا لهذه المدينة الواقعة على البحرالمتوسط ،سَعدنا بالمرافقة اللطيفة والهامة مع كل من السيد جعفر فرح والسيدة أسمهان عطوان ،والسينمائية غُلا طبري ،إضافة لحُسنِ ضيافة مركز مساواة الذي يُديره السيد جعفر ،كل هذا ،برفقة البروفسور منصورالذي أهدانا وقته الثمين وصورا يحتويها هذا الكتاب. ونشكر كذلك السيد نمر يزبك من الناصرة الذي أهدانا بعضاً من الصور من مجموعتهِ الخاصة التي يملكها.

لقد شكلتْ زيارتُنا انطلاقةَهذا المشروع ،حيث عِشنا حسن الاستقبال والمساعدة من كل من فايز السقا وعائدة سليفي وخالد السعدي ونواف أحمد والذين كانوا بمثابة دليل لنا في بيت لحم ورام الله والقدس رغم الاوضاع الصعبة التي كانت تعيشها الضفة الغربية آنذاك في نهاية يونيو حزيران عام 2014.
وشكراً لِمن ساهموا في الترجمة ،ونخص منهم السادة رفعت عطفة و خليل صدقة وعدنان الأيوبي الذين ترجموا النصوص من الاسبانية الى العربية. ونُعبرُ عن شكرنا واعترافا للبروفسورة كارمن رويث برافو التي تكفلتْ بترجمةِ النصوص العربية إلى الاسبانيةِ، وقدمت لنا صوراً ممتازةً من دار النشر التي تُديرُها كانتارابيا.

وساهمَ في هذا العمل، السيدة ماري سي.غونثالث فاييخو التي نشكرها جزيل الشكر على ذلك. ونقدم الشكر والامتنان لكل من ألبروفسور إيسائياس بارينيبيدا ومروان البوريني رئيس جمعية القدس الاسبانية الفلسطينية بمدريد وسفير فلسطين في اسبانيا السيد موسى عوده والذي منذ اللحظة الأولى لانطلاق مشروع هذا الكتاب كان يُشجعنا على تنفيذهِ والسيرِ إلى الأمام وقدم لنا المساعدة والأتصالات مع آخرين.
كما أن الثقةَ التي مَنحتها لنا دارالنشر اورينتي و ميديتيرانيو منذ بدايةِ التحضيرِ لهذا الكتاب وتضامن ومساهمة جمعية بلادي في اقليم الباسك ومؤسسة اراغواني في سانتياغو دي كومبوستيلا و لجنة التضامن مع القضيةِ العربيةِ في استورياس، مَكَّنتنا مِن إعدادِ ونشرِ هذا الكتاب ،فالشكر لهم جميعا.
والأمتنان الأكبر لأبناءِ فِلسطين،من الحاضر والماضي،ممن ظهروا في صُورِ هذا الكتاب ومِمَنْ لَمْ تشملهم صورُه.

ساندرا باريلارو و تيريسا أرانغورين

ضد المحو

ذاكرة صوَريّة لفلسطين ما قبل النكبة

حرّرها تيريسا أرانغورين وساندرا باريلارو

المقدمة بقلم محمد الكرد

H